THE LESSONS FROM APPRENTICE

TIME INC. HOME ENTERTAINMENT

Publisher Richard Fraiman

Executive Director, Marketing Services Carol Pittard

Director, Retail & Special Sales Tom Mifsud

Marketing Director, Branded Businesses Swati Rao

Director, New Product Development Peter Harper

Assistant Financial Director Steven Sandonato

Prepress Manager Emily Rabin

Book Production Manager Jonathan Polsky

Associate Prepress Manager Anne-Michelle Gallero

Special thanks: Victoria Alfonso, Bozena Bannett, Alexandra Bliss, Glenn Buonocore, Bernadette Corbie, Suzanne Janso, Robert Marasco, Brooke McGuire, Ilene Schreider, Adriana Tierno, Britney Williams

Published by Time Inc. Home Entertainment

Time Inc.

1271 Avenue of the Americas

New York, New York 10020

Produced by Downtown Bookworks Inc.

President Julie Merberg

Director Patty Brown

Editor Sara Newberry

Associate Editor Sarah Parvis

Written by Michael Robin

Design by Georgia Rucker Design

ISBN: 1-932994-26-2

Time Inc. Home Entertainment is a trademark of Time Inc.

We welcome your comments and suggestions about Time Inc. Home Entertainment. Please write to us at:

Time Inc. Home Entertainment

Attention: Book Editors

PO Box 11016

Des Moines, IA 50336-1016

If you would like to order any of our hardcover Collector's Edition books, please call us at 1-800-327-6388 (Monday through Friday, 7:00 a.m.–8:00 p.m. or Saturday, 7:00 a.m.–6:00 p.m. Central Time).

The Apprentice would like to thank: Mark Burnett, Conrad Riggs, Jay Bienstock, Kevin Harris, Roy Bank, Sue Guercioni, Laura Ambriz, Alan Blum, Shannon Sweeny, Keith Quinn, David Eilenberg, Ted Smith, Courtney Higgins, Heather Schuster, Chris Wilkas, Eda Benjakul, Brien Meagher, Dan Gill III, Brian Philo, Sadoux Kim, Frank Moultak, Tim Tevault, Jordan Yospe, James Sterling, Bernard Gugar, Junko Takeya, and Justin Hochberg

THE APPRENTICE

LESSONS FROM

SECRETS TO SUCCESS
from The Boardroom to The Business World

FOREWORD BY

Donald Trump

Time Inc.
HOME ENTERTAINMENT

WRITTEN BY MICHAEL ROBIN

LESSONS FROM THE APPRENTICE

CONTENTS

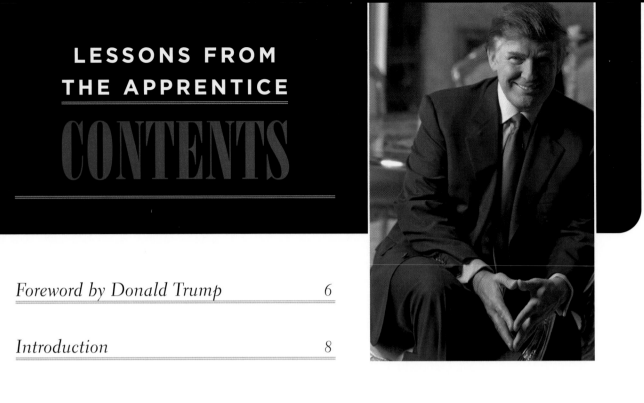

FOREWORD

I had been approached many times to appear in a reality show, but it wasn't until Mark Burnett came to me with his idea that I considered it. The reason is that *The Apprentice* has an educational subtext—it's not merely entertainment. There are lessons to be learned if viewers choose to pay attention on that level. That's what appealed to me, and that's what I think gives the show a substance that other shows may lack.

People comment on the variety of the tasks that we present to the participants. That's because business has many dimensions and to be successful one has to be able to operate effectively in many capacities. What may appear simple can actually be complex, and vice versa. I can tell a lot about someone by how he or she handles something seemingly simple. I need people who are able to focus, and remain focused, despite being in a maelstrom of activity. Can they maintain their equilibrium even in that environment?

Look at our winners Bill Rancic, Kelly Perdew, and Kendra Todd. That ability is one thing they all have in common: they kept their focus and their equilibrium and maintained a clear-sighted goal, which was to be the best, and to win. They were the best, and they won. Sometimes it's that simple.

What isn't so simple is something that's frequently overlooked when talking about business: passion. I firmly believe you have to love what you're doing in order to achieve long-lasting success. Passion gives great momentum and can be the catalyst for great achievement. That's another thing I look for in people, whether it's on the surface or not. It can make someone indomitable in the best sense of the word, and it's a way I can innately identify winners. *The Apprentice* serves as a very good interview process, and viewers can learn as much as the players. I've always believed that those who want to learn will learn, but the materials have to be made available to them. *The Apprentice* is of that substance, and the lessons are there for those who choose to pay attention.

I really don't want to see you in the boardroom, I'm busy enough already. So pay attention to the lessons presented to you on *The Apprentice* and in this book, and maybe we can avoid an unpleasant encounter. Keep your focus, maintain your momentum, and don't forget the passion!

Donald J. Trump

INTRODUCTION

When *The Apprentice* hit it really big on NBC in 2004, it wasn't hard to see why. Its leading man, Donald Trump, was already an icon, the embodiment of a certain kind of American dream. People all over the world knew the name, the voice, the hair. He left his stamp on his skyscrapers' faces, and his own face made books and newspapers fly off the stands whenever it appeared. He seemed to be the absolute paragon of success: ruthless, unforgiving, endlessly ambitious, and wealthy beyond mortal dreams. And yet whenever his fellow New Yorkers spotted The Donald they always gave him a wave rather than a Bronx cheer. Somehow he still seemed like one of us. He walked to work. He battled back from the brink of ruin in the '90s when everyone declared him finished. He had cool kids. He loved New York. And, best of all, he liked to have fun. While fellow moguls made their moves behind the scenes, Trump was out and about: enjoying the ball game, taking in the fashion show, hanging out with entertainers he admired. The man spent his money the way we would if we had it.

So when The Donald made his first appearance in the Trump Tower boardroom on *The Apprentice*'s premiere episode it felt good to see that we'd been right about him all along. Trump could be fearsome, but he also had a softer side. He seemed genuinely to like the people on the other side of the table, and not just the pretty ones. He pounced on mistakes but also poked fun at himself. The hair turned out to be his own. His self-promotion was so relentless that it became endearing. Viewers smiled when we heard the words "most luxurious" and "most successful." What's more, we eventually realized that Trump's hyperbolic language is part of what makes him great. In "the meanest city in the world," you never

stop working if you want to stay on top. Let others beware the naked man who offers you his shirt—The Donald would grab it and sell it at a nice markup.

Never let up. That's the lesson Donald Trump taught us, whether we knew it or not long before *The Apprentice* went on the air. Imagine what we can learn now that we have a window into Trump Tower's inner sanctum.

For better or worse, *The Apprentice* has already changed the way America goes about its business. It's hard to make it through the day without hearing "Step up to the plate," "Take accountability," or "Think outside the box." And for those who are serious about moving up in the business world, *The Apprentice* offers a chance to learn from the best.

The program has featured guest appearances by some of the world's most accomplished executives. Besides Trump, viewers heard words of wisdom from the likes of Rudy Giuliani, Steve Forbes, Michael Bloomberg, Donnie Deutsch, George Steinbrenner, and Alan "Ace" Greenberg. While applicants of *The Apprentice* put themselves through hell to learn what it takes to be Trump, millions of Americans accomplished just that without ever leaving the sofa.

The Thirteen-Week Job Interview

As the hopefuls converged on Trump Tower from all over the country, their new boss explained what they were in for:

"For the next thirteen weeks these sixteen candidates will embark on a unique job interview. They'll live together in a suite in Trump Tower, one of the great buildings of the world, right on Fifth Avenue. They'll be divided into two groups. Each week they'll compete against one another in a series of tasks. The winning team will continue to live in their suite; the losers will come to my boardroom, where someone is fired and sent home. It's either the suite or the street."

To be his eyes and ears while the applicants took on their tasks, Trump turned to two of his most trusted advisors: George Ross, Executive Vice President and Senior Counsel, and Carolyn Kepcher, Chief Operating Officer of one of his companies. The pair would report back to Trump when it was time to determine who deserved the credit and who deserved the blame.

CAROLYN KEPCHER

"She's tough. She's nasty. But she's also actually very nice." —Donald Trump

GEORGE ROSS

"He's also tough and nasty. And he's actually not very nice." —Donald Trump

To each task's victor went the spoils. Winners might find themselves at a table in one of New York's finest restaurants, or pulling up a chair for a tête-à-tête with Trump in his apartment. They might take to the air for a helicopter ride around Manhattan, or go all the way to Florida for a day at his magnificent club, Mar-a-Lago. An applicant might go up in the air and just float there, as did those who won a chance to experience weightlessness, or return to earth in disgrace after being shot down by a teammate in a simulated dogfight. Winners were serenaded by Billy Joel, and shook hands with great leaders such as Rudy Giuliani. The taste of Trump luxury was intoxicating.

Losers went to the boardroom. After a withering interrogation by Trump, George, and Carolyn, the losing project manager—and the two teammates he or she considered most responsible for the loss—stayed behind while the others went back to the safety of the suite. Those left in the boardroom fought for their lives against the executives—and against one another. If they did well, they were allowed to take the up elevator back to the suite and compete another day. If they didn't, Donald Trump pointed his finger and uttered the words no one wanted to hear: "You're fired." The disgraced applicant took the down elevator to the street, where he or she climbed into the back of a yellow taxi and vanished from the show.

Top Trump executives George Ross and Carolyn Kepcher are their boss's eyes and ears during the Apprentice tasks.

At the end of the thirteen-week interview, the sole remaining candidate would become the president of a Trump company, at a huge salary, for a period of one year. It would take tremendous guts, imagination, endurance, leadership, and guile to make it through to the end. But, most of all, it would take an understanding of what it means to do business the Trump way.

Thanks to *The Apprentice*, aspiring tycoons everywhere now share that understanding. Every episode came loaded with lessons on how to make it big—really big.

Let's review the curriculum that started with *The Apprentice*. (For a synopsis of each episode mentioned throughout the book, turn to page 144.)

"New York, my city, where the wheels of the global economy never stop turning. A concrete metropolis of unparalleled strength and purpose that drives the business world. Manhattan is a tough place. This island is the real jungle. If you're not careful it can chew you up and spit you out, but if you work hard you can really hit it big, and I mean really big."

—Donald Trump

CHAPTER 1

STARTING A BUSINESS

The expectations of the season one applicants brimmed when Mr. Trump called them onto the floor of the New York Stock Exchange for *The Apprentice*'s first-ever task assignment. Who knew what high-stakes challenge awaited them there in the heart of the financial universe? But to their surprise the applicants learned that they wouldn't be plunging into Wall Street's cauldron of money and power—they'd be plunging into lemon rinds and pulp as operators of old-fashioned lemonade stands.

Thus *The Apprentice* kicked off its inaugural episode with a twist to which it would return again and again: force a cast of eager overachievers to go back to basics and build brand-new businesses from humble

Season one's candidates look up to Trump from the New York Stock Exchange trading floor at the Lemonade Stand challenge's opening bell.

beginnings. Often the applicants themselves wound up humbled, as they relearned fundamental lessons that even enterprising children at lemonade stands ought to know. Right from the start, *The Apprentice* reminded us of the rules to bear in mind when seeking to launch a new venture into Wall Street's stratosphere.

What's in a Name?

Boys, girls, book smarts, street smarts . . . each team's first challenge is to come up with a winning name. In the season two premier, when Donald Trump heard that the men's team had named itself "Mosaic," his response was characteristically direct: "Wow, that's awful!" Not exactly what you want to hear when you announce yourself to the world. A name intended to evoke a dazzling collection of interknit talents instead left the competition in stitches. Even Raj, himself a Mosaic member, grumbled about the "fruity-toot" moniker.

In contrast, the season one women won Trump's nod of approval when they cannily dubbed themselves "Protégé." Before the first task had even begun, they'd clarified their purpose: to emulate and excel. That the name flattered their prospective boss probably didn't hurt, either.

A name is the first thing others learn about your new business—make sure it sends the right message.

> *"Trump is associated with the biggest and the best. If it has his name on it, it's something extraordinary. That's the stock-in-trade."*
> —George Ross

Location, Location, Location

- In season one's Lemonade Stand episode, Versacorp under Troy seemed unstoppable. Although the teams had been told to make a profit on the streets of New York with just $250 in seed money, the men made it look easy. While their female counterparts at Protégé struggled to organize, team Versacorp scouted locations and gathered supplies. Kwame even negotiated free materials from a local merchant. But none of it mattered when the men chose to peddle their wares in the sparsely populated Seaport, while the women found a busy street chock-full of leering suits. Though Versacorp began the day like a well-oiled machine, their failure to find a well-trafficked location cost them the victory.

David's people skills frighten off a rare customer at Versacorp's deserted lemonade stand location.

Kristi gives a customer a little extra sugar with his beverage at Mosaic's teeming table.

- Later on in season one, in the Flea Market episode, the teams were ordered to stock up tables with whatever goods they chose and go head to head in the cutthroat world of a New York neighborhood bazaar. The winds of fortune appeared to blow Protégé's way when a threatening sky made their inventory of umbrellas look even more inviting. Protégé project manager Kristi sensibly moved the team's table indoors, where the customers and goods could stay dry. But it was Kristi who was left high and dry when the clouds lifted and shoppers moved outdoors, where Nick's Versacorp crew sold everything down to—and including—the tablecloth. An umbrella saleswoman should never be undone by rain. How could Kristi have rolled with the meteorological punches? She could have employed one of these strategies, both of which were employed in season two:

Versacorp earns a group hug after a clear sky helps them clear out their entire inventory.

Relocation

Not every businessperson can easily pick up and go when a promising location sours, but Ivana could—and did—when an irate street vendor hassled her crew in the Ciao Bella episode. Things were looking up for Apex in their effort to be Times Square's highest-grossing ice-cream cart as theatergoers took a shine to their brand-new Red Velvet flavor. But a choice stretch of sidewalk is a prize worth fighting for if you make your living on the street, and the team soon found itself harangued by a food-cart operator who didn't think his intersection was big enough for two. Rather than squander time and resources on a conflict she couldn't win, Ivana chose the lesser of two evils and moved Apex's operation to another Times Square location with comparable traffic—and less competition.

They'd Rather Switch than Fight: Apex decides to move their ice-cream cart rather than duke it out with a territorial hot dog vendor.

Expansion

Sometimes it pays to trawl with a wider net. During the Doggie Business episode, in which teams had to start rival canine-oriented enterprises from scratch, Raj didn't like Apex's chances when most passersby at their Central Park grooming station turned out to be of the two-legged variety. Raj realized that if New York's widely dispersed dog owners weren't finding their way to Apex, then Apex should find its way to them. He convinced project manager Jennifer M. to split the team in half and open at a second location, and although business was modest there too, the two stations' combined profit exceeded that of Mosaic's one.

Find a Unique Product

A city that often seems to have a deli, pharmacy, coffee shop and a pizzeria on every block is the perfect place to learn the importance of standing out in a crowd. New Yorkers have a lot of choices, so only a product or service that is truly special is likely to attract eyeballs and dollars. Making the extra effort to offer something unique often made the difference on *The Apprentice*.

A Stitch in Time: Well-placed ribbons sew up Versacorp's Flea Market win.

- In season one's Flea Market episode, Kristi thought she had a winning approach when she purchased hats and umbrellas at rock-bottom prices in Chinatown, then sold them at a nice markup at her uptown table. But the profit margin proved meaningless when the goods failed to excite flea-market shoppers. Perhaps customers knew that better prices for the same products were just a few subway stops away. Meanwhile, Nick's Versacorp sewed fairly ordinary ribbons onto fairly ordinary T-shirts, and with just that little bit of extra effort generated a completely original look, and a nifty little profit.

Net Worth's trailer announces their innovation in bold letters.

- Season three's Business on Wheels episode found the teams with luxurious Airstream trailers and little else with which to start the new business of their choice. Though both teams had minimal seed money, one—Tana's Net Worth—proved rich in imagination when they dreamed up "Actor Factor," a sort of mobile casting couch in which performers could pay for an audience with an accredited New York casting director. It was a totally unique idea, and a profitable one in a city teeming with opportunity-starved thespians who proved more than willing to pony up the day's tips for a chance to be seen.

Meanwhile, at Magna's competing trailer, even the most effusive come-ons failed to excite enough interest in the team's tepid "City Spa" concept. Curbside back rubs and nail care couldn't quicken the pulses of customers who knew that these services are readily available in salons throughout the five boroughs.

The Apprentice demonstrates that the surest way to attract people who think they've seen it all is to prove them wrong.

Even unemployed actors get their own trailer thanks to Net Worth.

CHAPTER 2

BRAINSTORMING 101

"Thinking outside the box is something that is very much a cliché, but if you want to be successful, that's how you're going to have to do it."

—Donald Trump

Many *Apprentice* tasks were won or lost in their earliest hours, when teammates gathered to exchange the business world's most valuable currency: ideas. All the energy in the world couldn't save a team saddled with a stinker of an idea; Magna might as well have packed their bags for the boardroom on the spot when they left their Dove Cool Moisture brainstorming session declaring, "Let's make this vegetable porno the best vegetable porno we can possibly make." In contrast, Amy's Pedicab Fleet masterstroke—selling ads on the vehicles—relegated the day's receipts to mere icing on the cake; victory was in the bag before a single fare was sold. In season three, big business school brains meant nothing when street-smart creativity tipped the early episodes in Net Worth's favor, and throughout the series teams committed to bad ideas because they were the only ones available. So what's a project manager to do when inspiration goes on strike? *The Apprentice* held many examples of how to get—or inspire others to get—the "big idea."

Some of season one's crack creatives zero in on the Big Idea.

Troy's wild mind was boxed in by sharp but unimaginative teammates.

How Madeline DeVries Assembles the Right Team

Madeline DeVries founded DeVries Public Relations in 1978 and has since seen it prosper into one of the world's most successful and selective consumer marketing public relations agencies, with a client roster that includes Tupperware, Bank of America, and Procter & Gamble. Viewers met her in season two's Vanilla Mint Crest episode.

We get people from different parts of the agency together. If it's a new piece of business we try to get an unusual team of people with diverse experiences and knowledge, and we bring in outside people. It's our own brainpower and lots of years of experience with a tremendous amount of outside stimulation.

Assemble the Right Team

Team fortunes flew highest when the best personnel were on the launching pad. Leaders who brainstormed with imaginative colleagues were most likely to find a concept that won the task outright, while the rest often found that salesmanship and grit carry you only so far.

- No wonder project manager Bill was the big idea beneficiary in the Pedicab Fleet episode: he brainstormed with Amy and Katrina, who had earned reputations for creativity, while rival project manager Troy traded ideas with Kwame and Heidi, who had not. Surrounded by talented but largely conventional thinkers, Troy pedaled in place all episode long.

- "I am guilty of having pushed forward the only thing that was on the table," said Raj, explaining his role in Apex's decisive NYPD Recruitment loss, and it's easy in hindsight to see why the table was bare. Although the team was loaded with strong-willed players—Chris R., Ivana, Jennifer M., Kevin, and Raj—a look at the record reveals few ideas, aside from Ivana's Levi's Catalogue "fit wheel," that anyone would characterize a "outside the box." A team packed with talent in every other area had nothing to offer project manager Elizabeth when her own imagination failed. Examine past performance carefully when choosing a brainstorming lineup.

Take a Brainstorming Breather

"The meetings have to be fun and they can't be too long. Maybe an hour. It takes fifteen minutes to get grounded and then what comes out is usually the jewels. Sometimes you can over-think something and it's better to stop and come back and do it again."

—Madeline DeVries

Managing Creativity

Apprentice brainstorming sessions frequently looked like free-for-alls, with wild notions being aired with abandon and white paper flip charts covered with illegible scrawls. Closer examination, however, reveals how a savvy manager makes the most of the idea whirlwind.

Stand by Your Flip Chart

In the right hands, an easel and a pad of white paper turned into subtle tools for managing conference-room conversations. Many project managers used their black markers like conductor's batons to draw out the things they wanted to hear. Some listed each and every idea and then winnowed; others sketched, underlined, and decorated to point their teams in the desired direction. Angie even threw in a patriotic march and snappy salute to muster enthusiasm for her political debate idea in the Nescafé Taster's Choice episode; although her lyrics weren't exactly Pulitzer material—"Choose Nescafé today! . . . Everybody say 'Hey!'"—she left no doubt about her commitment to her concept. With their performances at the flip chart, good leaders established order amid the brainstorming chaos.

Linda Sawyer on Productive Brainstorming

Linda Sawyer, Deutsch Inc.'s Managing Partner and Chief Operating Officer, helped Donnie Deutsch turn his agency into an industry leader.

You need to create an environment where you inspire people to think completely out of the box, to feel comfortable putting themselves on the line and that there's no stupid idea or question. I think at the same time brainstorming sessions need a strong leader that can keep reining the conversation so that you're moving ahead and not all over the place. Someone who inspires people to come up with a crazy idea which would never work in the real world. But after that crazy idea comes a really smart idea. A solution.

Angie comes up with the idea that will win the task for Net Worth.

Why Linda Sawyer Flips for Flip Charts

I think the reason you see a lot of flip charts is that it happens to be a very good tool. Once you get to a good idea, you take pause, agree that this thing we've come up with is a smart building block, and put that piece on the board. And then you use that as a building block to get to the next phase and then as you lay it out, all of a sudden, lo and behold, you have all these blocks that hopefully build to a big idea.

Sometimes if we don't land but we know we're in this really good place where there's a lot of fertile ground and we've come up with a lot of great ideas, we'll leave the sheet hanging in a room so it inspires [the team] to keep thinking about it.

Bill waits to hear a winner.

Audrey stews after Kristen's slight.

Create a Safe Space

Season one winner Bill always let his teammates know it was okay to let their imaginations run wild. As Katrina suggests several bad ideas near the start of the Pedicab Fleet episode, Bill's carefully neutral face and body language are the marks of an effective listener. Katrina knows her ideas haven't clicked, but also that it's safe to try again. Look at Kristen in the Dove Cool Moisture episode for a model of what not to do. As Net Worth tries to brainstorm a body-wash buzz builder, she responds to Audrey's idea with a dismissive "No offense, I want something original." Kristen's body language is worse still: she doesn't even bother to look up as she delivers her dis. Audrey is, of course, slammed into silence and Net Worth is on course for a loss.

Isolate Energy Vampires

Michael was sure that the way to generate excitement for Nescafé Taster's Choice was to have European models serve it on the street. So certain was he that after his fellow Magnas shot the idea down, Michael devoted himself to returning the favor. Secure in his exemption, Michael mocked his colleagues' contributions and poisoned the morale of a team already at a loss for an exciting concept. Something had to be done. Project manager Danny tried to send a message with humor ("Mike, if you need a time-out in the corner let me know, okay?") and, when that failed, with directness ("Mike, I want you to stop talking about the promotion"). Danny's intervention brought on an abusive tirade, but it stemmed the negativity enough for Magna to move on.

Wait for the Big One

Sheer quantity of ideas is useless without a leader who can recognize a winner. The superior project managers refused to settle for anything less than the best idea, and knew it when they heard it.

- Again, watch Bill in the Pedicab Fleet episode. At first he takes in Katrina's barrage of so-so suggestions with professional neutrality. Then when the red-hot idea comes, he takes decisive action. The instant Amy suggests selling advertising on the vehicles, Bill terminates the brainstorming session and throws the whole team into making the strategy work. "If we put this together it will be a bloodbath," he predicts. He's right on the money.

> *"People settle for mediocrity for one reason: they're lazy. I've seen it so often. People go into something, they don't want to go that extra step. They know it's not gonna be great. It might be good, it might be okay—it's not gonna be great."*
>
> —Donald Trump

Net Worth's visionaries on their way to advertising infamy in the Dove Cool Moisture episode.

Meanwhile, over at Protégé project manager Troy goes with his own prepaid rickshaw ride card as the idea that will seal the win. An outside-the-box thinker if ever there was one, Troy fails to stretch his imagination just when he needs it most. The ride card flops, and in the boardroom he concedes that the task was lost in its opening hour: "Our idea was great," he admits, "theirs was brilliant."

- Evidence that it's smart not to turn off the tap too soon came in the Ciao Bella episode, when Kevin's eleventh-hour off-the-cuff suggestion saved the day for Apex. At the time, the team teetered on oblivion's lip as the deadline for inventing an ice cream flavor loomed but inspiration did not. Kevin knew it was time to make a choice . . . any choice. He told his teammates to drop a candy bar or doughnut in vanilla ice cream and call it a day. You could almost see the lightbulb go off over Wes's head. In that moment, Donut Ice Cream—and Apex's first win—was born. Because they didn't get behind a mediocre idea early, the team was open to a better one that arrived late. "You could put dog feces in that ice cream and it's gonna taste good," declared Pamela, proving that it's smart to turn off the tap eventually.

Bad Ads

"The regular typical thirty-second commercial doesn't cut it anymore," proclaimed legendary adman Donnie Deutsch at the beginning of the Dove Cool Moisture task. "I want you to blow me away in terms of 'Wow, this is different, I have to watch this.'" When it was all over, the teams had turned in advertisements that were indeed impossible to look away from, in the same way that it must have been impossible to take one's eyes off the *Titanic* as it went under. After screening the screamingly awful efforts, Donnie gave them two thumbs way down. "You both missed big," he said. "You both sucked." For the first time, a task had no winner at all. How did two talented squads with access to state-of-the-art facilities turn in work that was as watchable as a highway wreck? Disaster's seeds lay in the brainstorming sessions that started it all.

"We're not gonna win by being safe," said Bren as he proposed a story line in which a handsome restaurant worker

Linda Sawyer on the Dove Debacle

Talk about a good example of bad ads. There absolutely was no connection. The irony to me is a brand like Dove stands for purity, cleanliness, wholesomeness. Both those ads ended up being completely gratuitous and downright inappropriate for the brand. I think they fell in love with their own ideas. I think they weren't responsibly trying to sell a product with any kind of accountability. I think they were trying to be sensational and get a lot of attention and having a grand old time at their own expense. Or I should say at Dove's expense.

Erin gets her hands dirty during Magna's Dove debacle.

fondles a cucumber with a female colleague before breaking her heart by walking off with his male lover. Even Michael, Magna's king of inappropriate behavior, knew the idea was wrong for a widely sold product. "Would Dove appreciate it?" he wondered, "I don't think so." George Ross agreed. "It's a bad idea," growled the G-man. "Magna's going down the wrong path." How, then, did the worst small-screen idea since *Cop Rock* make it out of the conference room? Blame Erin. Magna's project manager appeared less interested in generating viable ideas than ogling actors' abs. "Scrubbing's hard work," she crowed as she cheerily lathered up her leading man for the camera. It wasn't until later that she realized Magna's opus looked like low-budget adult entertainment. By then it was too late. Erin had settled for a bad idea and now she was stuck with it. When Deutsch Managing Partner Valda Febo saw the final result, she said "Magna's campaign basically had a guy leaving with a guy and a woman left with a cucumber. I'm not sure as a woman I'm really excited about that." Trump's evaluation was more merciless still. "I thought it was the worst commercial I'd ever seen," he later said. "Until I saw Net Worth's ad."

"Our main goal is to make that guy laugh as hard as he can," said John as he outlined a joke about a marathon runner using Dove Cool Moisture to help him win the race. "He laughs and we win." Unfortunately for Net Worth, their own race was lost in the starting block. Although project manager Kristen would later admit, "No one understood the joke thing," she cut off discussion before it had really begun and stalked into the soundstage like advertising's Ed Wood. With so little on the table, Kristen flayed whatever humor there was from John's bare-bones idea. "This is so [bleep]ing in the box, this is right in the middle of the [box]," agonized Audrey, adding, in case we'd missed her point, "This *is* the box." The box became more like a coffin when Kristen actually cut the water out of an ad for a bath product. Carolyn cringed when she watched the runner scrub his face with commingled body wash and sweat. "It was disgusting," she said. "It repelled you from buying this product."

"*Ay ay ay*," winced The Donald, at a rare loss for words after viewing the ad that unsold the product. Bungled brainstorming had produced a memorable episode that each and every applicant would rather forget.

From the Mouths of Babes

With her caustic comments about critical kids, project manager Pamela made a mockery of Mattel's focus group in the Child's Play episode. Apex's effort at Crustacean Nation building was complete and the group watched from behind a two-way mirror as a roomful of six- to eight-year olds pronounced judgment. When one tiny skeptic acted indifferent, Pamela did the grown-up thing: she made fun of his haircut. "Look at that," she chuckled. "He looks like a mini *Dumb and Dumber*." While Pamela honed her schoolyard bully chops, Mattel executives watched the children carefully. Their lack of enthusiasm made a big difference when the time came to choose a winner. "In this business, you always want the kids to steer you," explained Mattel's Mark Sullivan as he awarded Mosaic the prize. Had Apex's Harvard and Wharton graduates paid more attention to their littlest customers, they might have learned a thing or two. Good ideas can come from anywhere.

Chris and John W. are a little uneasy about Pamela's focus-group commentary.

CHAPTER 3

THE NATURAL: DEVELOPING GOOD BUSINESS INSTINCTS

"I've always felt that my best deals were made with my instinct, not anything else."

—Donald Trump

Good leaders went into their *Apprentice* tasks with a well-thought-out plan. The best leaders knew how to change course when those plans ran into trouble. Applicants like season one's Troy McClain displayed an uncanny instinct for sealing deals with inspired improvisations just when things looked the worst. He and others who thought on their feet were more likely to land on them in the boardroom. Following their examples arms attentive viewers with skills that come in handy anytime, anywhere. Those of us born without the gifts of a Trump or a Troy can still learn how to recognize opportunity in adversity.

> *"The big thing in negotiation is to try and figure out your opponent. Otherwise you're going to look like an idiot, and lose big."*
>
> —Donald Trump

Troy's Boise drawl charms Russell Simmons.

Jessie's slow-talking irritates Isaac Mizrahi.

Read the Client's Cues

Protégé seemed on the verge of losing big when they didn't connect with entertainment impresario Russell Simmons in the Celebrity Auction episode. The task required them to get five stars to offer experiences to bidders in a Sotheby's auction for the Elizabeth Glaser Pediatric AIDS Foundation. Unfortunately, the team bogged down on its very first pitch. Although he felt uncharacteristically anxious about meeting a man he idolized, Kwame went into Mr. Simmons's office confident that one of Protégé's carefully considered ideas would click. Instead, every one flopped. Omarosa tried to come to the rescue, but Simmons only got crankier. On the sidelines, Troy realized Russell was responding as much to Kwame's and Omarosa's stiff deliveries as to their ideas. So he laid the drawl on thick and jumped into the conversation. The ice broke the minute Simmons heard the Boise boy's accent. Soon he was poking good-natured fun at Troy while the two hammered out an agreement. "Troy's a great closer," admitted Kwame. "His country demeanor helped close the deal."

In contrast, Troy's teammate Jessie completely failed to read Isaac Mizrahi's cues when their negotiation headed south. As Jessie ticked off ideas in a tone usually reserved for toddlers or pets, the celebrated designer's expression indicated his impatience, then his incredulousness. Still Jessie droned on. Finally Mizrahi could take no more. "I love how you're speaking to me as though I, like, have never spoken the English language," he said as the discussion ground to a halt. Jessie's failure to change course despite unmistakable signs that her approach was failing nearly left Protégé high and dry. Although Troy once again saved the day with upbeat energy and ideas that were in line with Mizrahi's clearly indicated enthusiasms, Jessie had made herself look like the team's weakest link.

"The time to back off is only when you're in the final discussions. When you're first throwing something on the table, go for broke, go for the sky. You throw it out and see what happens. If somebody said to you 'How much would you pay me for this house?' what are you gonna do, give 'em a high offer? You give 'em a low offer."

—George Ross

- John G.'s swagger, boardroom composure, and persuasive Burger King victory made him the candidate to beat in season three, until tone deaf negotiations in the Musician Experience episode earned him a well-deserved exit. The teams had been told to arrange experiences with some of the music world's biggest stars and then auction them on live TV. When project manager Chris S. handed artists like Fat Joe and Gene Simmons to Net Worth's bona fide musician, it seemed like the task was in the bag. But John blew it. He bored his clients with stories about himself. He sidelined teammates Erin and Stephanie with sexist insults ("It's time to pimp some girls!"). But worst of all he negotiated for unimaginative experiences—even when the performer clearly indicated they'd give more. "If you wanted to get the highest bid you want it to be

John's wallet chain—and ideas—failed to impress Jordan Pundik of New Found Glory.

"Negotiation is a very delicate art. Sometimes you have to be tough, sometimes you have to be as sweet as pie. I've always said that negotiation is not really learned—it's almost in the genes. A negotiator is born."

— Donald Trump

unique," said a New Found Glory member who was unimpressed by John's house party idea, "So is this special enough?" Gene Simmons made it even clearer: "I want mine to be bigger than theirs," he insisted. But John ignored his clients' signals and kept his sights aimed right where they started: low. When Net Worth lost the bidding war to a Magna team that had been audacious enough to ask for week-long experiences from Moby and Lil' Kim, there was no doubt who was responsible for the defeat. "John, why didn't you put on your list something that they could back off of?" asked George Ross. "Gene Simmons gave you the opportunity. He says 'I wanna be number one.'" But John, who'd talked incessantly rather than read the clients' cues, had finally fallen silent.

Identify the Obstacle

It took more than country charm to solve Protégé's woes in the Trump Ice episode. Manhattan merchants proved tough nuts to crack as spring water sales trickled out a case or two at a time. Neither Omarosa's smooth talk nor Amy's alluring numbers persuaded purchasers to think big. Finally Troy had what he called a "moment of clarity." The problem, he realized, wasn't price or product or marketing . . . the problem, familiar to anyone who's ever rented a New York apartment, was space. Customers couldn't take large shipments of water because they simply had nowhere to put it. All the persuasive selling in the world couldn't add square footage to cramped shops. Once the real obstacle was identified, Troy could set his inventive intelligence upon it and divine a solution. "We're missing the boat," he told his teammates, "we don't have to just do a one-time delivery." Soon Troy sewed up deals for just-in-time delivery of small orders over several consecutive weeks. Versacorp was crushed and Troy's star shone bright in the boardroom. "Watching him adapt tells me a lot about his personality," said Amy as she sized up a competitor who proved more formidable with every passing task. "He reads people well to figure out what tactic sells best. . . . He's doing a damn good job."

Gene Simmons preferred John G.'s "fluffer" to her overbearing partner.

Go to the Bullpen

Never be too proud to ask for help. Applicants who sent out a timely SOS when well-laid plans threatened to run off the rails were likeliest to get tasks back on track.

- "This task is going to be very important to Mr. Trump," said project manager Sandy in the Home Improvement episode, "Real estate is very near and dear to his heart." Determined to impress The Donald, Sandy was shattered when her contractor fell behind early in Mosaic's effort to raise a home's assessed value more than rival Apex. Sandy wept as team morale plummeted. "They were starting to smell defeat," she later admitted. Everyone, that is, but Andy. Mosaic's youngest member refused to throw in the towel and instead went out and found someone to throw in the trowel. When a passing contractor slowed to ask about the renovation work, Andy took his measure and invited him in. Soon the house swarmed with new workers—and new attitudes. Revitalized, Mosaic charged to victory.

Andy's relief team spruces up Mosaic's curb appeal.

Tara and Chris are waiting in the wings when Angie falters.

- Sometimes all it takes is matching the right staffer with the task. In the Business on Wheels episode, Net Worth put Angie, a former actress, in charge of finding a casting director for the team's innovative Actor Factor concept. Two and a half hours ticked by while Angie thumbed through the yellow pages without success. Finally, her teammates intervened. Tara, the idea's originator, got on the phone and, with help from Chris and John, reeled in a casting director pronto. Net Worth had all the right ingredients on hand—Tara's charm, Chris and John's negotiation skills—it just took a while to find the right recipe. Rather than watch Angie lose the game, they went to the bullpen and let Tara pitch the save.

Have a Plan B

The most effective problem solving happens before the task is underway. Teams that went into battle with contingency plans in hand coped best when trouble came.

- For example, Andy convinced Mosaic that a chance to win a million dollars was the perfect way to hype the debut of Procter & Gamble's Vanilla Mint Crest toothpaste, but when lawyers pulled the giveaway's plug at 2:30 A.M. the night before, it appeared he'd steered the team into a dead end. "When the group voted to do it, we put our eggs, chickens, we put the whole damn pen in this basket," agonized Pamela. Fortunately, the team hadn't quit working after committing to Andy's plan. They'd arranged for circus artists to perform at the giveaway, so when plan A flatlined, these entertainers became the main event. Mosaic enlivened things with three separate five thousand dollar prizes, but those were just icing on the cake. Fire-eaters and stilt-walkers thrilled adults and children alike with interactive performances, and the event was a big success. Because they had a fallback plan in place, Andy and company survived a brush with toothpaste disaster.

Who needs a million dollars? A circus saves Mosaic's day.

Madeline DeVries on Having a Plan B . . . and C . . . and D . . .

You have to be flexible. Changes have to take place all the time. You have to do it for the right reason: because you've picked up a new bit of information or you see eyes are turning to a whole other show or a whole other media outlet. It depends on being in the right place: where the consumer is looking. Not the place where the company thinks they should be.

No such safety net awaited Todd, Magna's project manager in the Burger King episode. He had delegated marketing and promotions to Danny, the team's self-described whiz in those departments, but as the day wore on and no concepts materialized, Todd began to worry. "Danny has been really erratic, going off on tangents, very hard to rein in," he remarked. Todd's worst fears were realized when Danny finally showed up with his horrific "Triple Play" ball toss. Unfortunately for Magna, they had no alternative. "Todd should have taken control of marketing when he saw that we had a problem," said Kendra, the only applicant to see things the same way as Trump, Carolyn, and George. "When something isn't working you go to plan B. You have to have a plan B." The tip came too late to save Todd, who had the dubious distinction of being the first season three participant to hear the words "You're fired."

CHAPTER 4

BRINGING A NEW PRODUCT TO MARKET

W hen it comes to brands, what's old is new again in the right hands. Such is the lesson learned from established companies that used *The Apprentice* to launch products that kept them on the cusp of consumer culture. Applicants who reaped rewards took on such tasks with eyes wide open to their customers' desires; those who did not often embarrassed themselves. Well-chosen products and marketing strategies made venerable brands seem cutting edge. One miscalculation, however, and they seemed worn out and irrelevant. Here are some of the ways in which the *Apprentice* applicants perfumed product launches with the heady aroma of success.

What's That Buzz?

"Buzz is the shorthand for a lot of exposure for a brand. Buzz engages people to start talking about a product, about a situation, about a personality. That's what every marketer wants: a lot of people talking about their brand."

—Madeline DeVries

Find the Right Packaging

Consumers judge books by their covers. A hot product won't leave the shelves if its wrapper's a turnoff. When Pepsi's chief marketing officer, Dave Burwick, challenged Apex and Mosaic to design a bottle and promotion for his company's new cola, Pepsi Edge, one team hit the bull's-eye and the other shot itself in the foot. A comparison of their final products offers hints on how to dress a new product for success.

Apex's design spelled it out for consumers—literally: the bottle was a stylish E-D-G-E and it had just about everything you want in a new product's package. Its unique look provided a striking visual that was bound to catch consumers' eyes. It matched the Pepsi brand's youthful appeal. It conveyed unmistakable product information in its lettered body. And by leaving a hole clear through the letter D, project manager Kelly improved functionality with a space in which to leave promotional materials. When Apex made its presentation before an amphitheater full of Pepsi marketers, the audience leaned forward for a better look. Apex's E-D-G-E design spelled victory.

The Pepsi Edge episode was the only time anyone ever complained about Jennifer M.'s hourglass shape. In this case, the shape belonged to the bottle she endorsed for Protégé's geography-themed bottle. The design had no fizz, but project manager Andy opted for it anyway. Naturally, the presentation was flatter than old cola. By the time Andy, apparently mistaking Pepsi for the Boy Scouts, wrapped his pitch by exclaiming "And on top of this is, most exciting, a navigational cap with compass!", viewers had a pretty good idea whom they'd see in the boardroom that night. The post-presentation discussion sounded more like a roast. On striking visuals: "That . . . looks like two blobs of a badly colored tennis ball." On matching Pepsi's youthful image: "I don't remember the last time geography was cool." On conveying product information: "It's wrapped, so you don't even know that there's a cola in there." The Donald on improved functionality: "Maybe you use this as a barbell." Protégé had imagined a travel award for their promotion's winners, but the only one who needed a suitcase was the episode's loser: Andy.

Ivana wipes away tears of joy when Apex's bottle gives them a clear Edge.

Jennifer M. can't even fake a smile over Mosaic's bulging bottle.

Scout the Terrain

Former intelligence officer Kelly could have taught his fellow applicants a thing or two about the value of good reconnaissance. Teams that educated themselves about their products, but not about the neighborhoods in which they wished to sell them, made mammoth goofs.

- Apex had what Stacy R. called "the best location in Times Square," from which to sell their Red Velvet Ice Cream in the Ciao Bella episode. And the location by the TKTS discount theater ticket booth did in fact seem ideal . . . until a furious hot dog vendor broke the news that they'd stolen his spot. Not only did he have a prior claim on the street corner, he had a city permit to sell there. Both the vendor and the need for a permit took Apex unawares.

    Ivana tried to rally with a fast relocation, but again the team's lack of familiarity with Times Square came back to bite them. The "Crossroads of the World" is not a difficult place to navigate, unless you confuse Broadway with Seventh Avenue as Apex did after their two ice-cream carts got separated. This out-of-towner howler turned reuniting the group into a time-consuming search-and-rescue operation despite the fact that the two carts were unwittingly within view of each other the whole time. Needless to say, a little research and a simple map would have spared Apex a world of embarrassment.

- Just two episodes later, the women of Apex repeated their mistake. Their restaurant opening was an elegant affair, with the team decked out in formal dresses amid upscale decor. Unfortunately, as Carolyn later pointed out, it was exactly the wrong vibe. "It's not a chic neighborhood," she admonished project manager Jennifer C. "If you look at the people who walk up and down the streets they're in blue jeans and T-shirts." A clear-eyed look outside the restaurant door might have rescued Apex from a third straight loss. Instead, as Carolyn said, "You all looked gorgeous. The restaurant looked gorgeous. It was wrong."

"New York is the big leagues. It's entirely different. Everything is accelerated. Whatever has been done elsewhere is done bigger and better and first in New York. So you have to be prepared to operate on a level above any other level you ever operated on."

—George Ross

- That some applicants were out of touch with New York City became clear during Protégé's Vanilla Mint Crest brainstorming session. First John suggested contaminating the Hudson with toothpaste-colored foam, a real jaw-dropper in a city that's spent decades trying to get its rivers back to a color that at least remotely resembles water. But viewers who thought John had sewed up the title of Most Clueless San Franciscan hadn't reckoned on Pamela. Said she: "If we could create the aroma of vanilla and pump it into the subway systems, that's something that everybody would talk about." She left out " . . . at the Department of Homeland Security." When an idea's so bad it might get you sent to Guantánamo, it's time to rethink your approach.

"When I build a building or when I build a golf course or a club or whatever I do, you always have to go after a certain audience. You have to be able to pinpoint your market, and if you don't pinpoint the market, you won't be successful."

—Donald Trump

Know Your Market

Tana and Kendra marched to season three's finale by going three-for-three in tasks that involved established companies bringing new products to market. They didn't just win, they won big; in at least two cases the companies adopted the women's creations for mass production. It's hard to say which was more astonishing: their success, or their competition's inability to catch on. Consider:

Tana and Kendra show why they were the final two applicants of season three.

- In the American Eagle episode, Magna and Net Worth were required to create a wearable technology clothing line. Magna's Tana and Kendra marched straight to a store and quizzed shoppers about the gizmos they use and the features they'd like to see. Meanwhile, Net Worth trusted that Alex's "metrosexual" instincts were all they needed to guide their designs. They were wrong. When during Net Worth's presentation an American Eagle executive asked what device was most important to their customers, Angie didn't know for sure. "An iPod?" she suggested unconvincingly. Magna, on the other hand, had all the right answers (American Eagle buyers love their cell phones!) thanks to Tana and Kendra.

Kendra and Tana focus on the client's needs once again, ensuring a third straight victory for Magna.

- History repeated itself on the next task when Magna's project manager, Kendra, parked a Pontiac Solstice in public and let the reactions of passersby steer her toward the "love affair with a car"-themed brochure that would bowl over GM execs. Net Worth once again dispensed with market research, and once again turned in a pallid effort that won them only scorn.

- Why fix it if it ain't broke? For the third consecutive episode, Magna scored big with a focus group after Staples asked them to invent a new clutter-reducing office product. Tana and Kendra pawed through shopping carts and picked brains at Staples stores to learn what office managers were buying, and the result, now known as the Staples Desk Apprentice, proved popular first with the task's judges and later with the buying public. Sure enough, over at Net Worth a few futile phone calls were all the research Bren and Alex managed to do before going ahead with an impractical mobile desk unit that no one wanted.

If past episodes of *The Apprentice* hadn't made clear the importance of knowing your market, these three erased any doubt. The men of Net Worth were the only ones who somehow missed the message.

Bren struggles to get an office manager to take his call in the Staples episode.

CHAPTER 5

HOW TO STAY AHEAD OF THE COMPETITION

M ore often than not, *Apprentice* teams were evenly matched. Each side had its leaders, workhorses, live wires, and loose cannons. The margin between defeat and victory was frequently slim. Small strategic choices could pay off big-time at the finish. Here are some of the ways in which winners opened up a lead— and kept it.

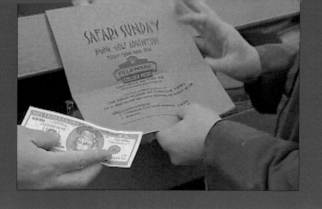

Kendra's exclusive deal with Chelsea Piers put Safari Sunday flyers in the right hands.

Protect the Winning Idea

- Bill knew that the key to Casino victory lay in registering the Trump Taj Mahal's VIP gamblers at Protégé's table. Just as important, he realized that he had to stop Amy's Versacorp team from adopting the same strategy once they caught wind of it. So Bill negotiated for the exclusive right to escort the VIPs straight from their check-in line to Protégé's registration area. Sure enough, Amy saw the value in Bill's tactic and sent models to lure VIPs her way. But Bill shooed them off, per his agreement with the house. Protecting his idea proved as crucial as having it in the first place.

- Likewise, Kendra made a deal with Chelsea Piers that made Magna the only team permitted to leave discount flyers for its miniature golf course on the premises. Despite Net Worth's clown suits, more customers came Magna's way—and many of them had Kendra's flyers in hand. By keeping the competition out of the nearby sports complex, Kendra sank a hole in one.

- A security leak nearly melted the Mosaic men's chance of winning the Ciao Bella task. The team wrote out a clever plan to sell their Donut Ice Cream in Times Square, then left it sitting out in the open in the suite. Naturally, the Apex women helped themselves. An effortless act of corporate espionage ensured that there'd be two teams working Times Square the next day. The men still won, but it would have been a lot easier if they'd kept their good ideas away from prying eyes.

Make a Good Presentation

Some competitions were decided by dollars: whichever team rang up the most sales was the winner. In others, the client's executives made the call. In the latter case, teams presented to top businesspeople (sometimes an auditorium full of them!) and if something was out of place they were sure to hear about it—on the spot or in the boardroom. Here's how some competitors helped or hindered themselves at the finish line.

Coordinate

- The Protégé women were on the same page—and in the same outfits—when they wowed Donnie Deutsch and his clients with their racy ideas for the Marquis Jet Card. Matching flight attendant uniforms sent the message that the team had its act together, and the well-rehearsed salesmanship of Omarosa, Heidi, and Amy proved it.

- What's a sure way to turn off a roomful of Levi's executives? Mosaic found out when they showed up for their Levi's Catalogue presentation in another company's jeans! "What's up with that?" asked Levi's prez Robert Hanson. Sure enough, the clueless crew turned out to be just as out of sync between the ears as below the waist. Maria got in the judges' faces with groaners like "If being sexy is wrong, I don't wanna be right" while her teammates winced. "The only thing I'd say to you is 'Plan ahead next time,'" coached Hanson as Mosaic braced themselves for the boardroom.

> *"In life you can have a great idea, but if you can't get those ideas across it's never ever going to work. I know so many people who have great ideas, but they can't sell the ideas. Guess what, they're not successful."*
>
> —Donald Trump

Linda Sawyer on the Art of the Presentation

I think you need to tell a story and you need to tell it in a very focused, clear, succinct way. And, just like a good story, there's a beginning, a middle, and an end and a good plot. Establish up front what you're trying to accomplish and then in a very linear, clear way deliver those objectives. And ultimately you want to end with a "Here's how and why it will work."

Protege presented a united front in matching flight attendant uniforms.

Never Let 'Em See You Sweat

- Apex probably lost a few points during their Levi's Catalogue presentation when Kevin came down with the worst flop sweat since Nixon debated Kennedy. Either Kevin was under-rehearsed or he'd just downed a bushel of jalapeños. It was hard to tell if we were seeing performance jitters or a hot flash. Apex weathered the flood, but they could have spared themselves an awkward moment by putting only their best pitchers into the rotation.

Kevin, Kelly, and Ivana put the finishing touches on Apex's Levi's catalogue.

- One of the best clutch pitchers was Jennifer M., who in the QVC TV episode became Apex's spokeswoman on live TV with only a moment's notice. Jennifer filled Maria's shoes without batting an eye after Pamela demoted Maria for batting hers too often. In contrast to Maria's unnerving intensity, Jennifer's relaxed tone and body language made her look and sound like a pro—not like a lawyer who'd been conscripted just moments before. Jennifer proved it was no accident in the Levi's Catalogue episode when she modeled jeans for the team's photographers as if she had been born to do it. Watching Jennifer work, Ivana displayed her knack for back-handed compliments by noting, "She can manipulate her persona in any way, and that's what you want in a model." And, she might have added, an exceptional presenter.

Jennifer M. exhibits her calm and collected demeanor in front of the camera.

Harmonize

- Tana was nervous before Magna's pitch to American Eagle Outfitter's executives, and with good reason: her teammates, Kendra and Craig, had battled all episode long. "Well, this is great," Tana said. "I got two teammates that are at each other's throat, hate each other, infuriate each other, and now we have to give a great presentation." She needn't have worried. Whatever their differences, Kendra and Craig knew when to put the team first. "Even though he's an ass, one thing that Craig and I share in common is that we want to win," Kendra explained. "And therefore we were able to put on a happy face. It's kind of like faking a marriage that went bad years ago." The pair's performance, like their product, was superb. Bad blood didn't get in the way of good business.

- Net Worth's disarray undid Angie in that same episode. It was a case of the right hand not knowing what the left was doing when the team set out for its pitch late and with no one in charge of bringing the clothes they were supposed to present. When a model left an important jacket behind, Angie unraveled. Blame for Net Worth's disharmony rightfully belonged at project manager Alex's feet, but it was Angie, the presenter, who took the fall when she choked in front of the judges.

The loss of key clothes caused Angie to unravel.

Adverbs Are Not Your Friends

The deck was stacked against Chris S. when he presented Net Worth's mediocre Pontiac Solstice brochure to General Motors execs who'd just been bowled over by Kendra's eye-catching and heartstring-tugging entry. But he did nothing to dispel the impression that he was in over his head when he opened his pitch with an assault upon the mother tongue. Although words like "interiorly" and "exteriorly" were more entertaining than anything Bren had put on the page, they let the judges know that Net Worth was a bad fit for a project that was all about communication.

The Madeline DeVries Guide to the Perfect Presentation

1) Do Your Homework: Way before you make a presentation, know that category and, more specifically, where your client's brand is within that category and what they want to do. Our teams know as much as their counterparts on the client's side.

2) Be Fresh: Bring something new and then be very clear about it. It doesn't help if I tell you, "I'm going to get you a lot of publicity." That has no substance to it. How are you going to get it, why are you going to get it, and what's the big idea about it?

3) Rehearse: I've made I couldn't even count how many presentations in my life—I still rehearse every single thing that I'm going to say with a group so we become one team representing a lot of facets of some big ideas in a program. We have to glue ourselves together so that we are sure that we can say it—and do it once the client says yes.

4) Make It Beautiful: It's got to be visually fabulous. I'd rather put one word up than a slide with lots of bullets. Say, "Here's the one or the three most important objectives"—don't sit there with a list of ten. Nobody's going to solve ten objectives all at once. In a presentation format, you want to hit the most important things.

5) Make It Quick: The worst thing is if it's boring.

Don't Waste Waste

Donald Trump saved millions when he bought a first-rate jet that had been mothballed in the Nevada desert. His example should have clued his potential apprentices into the savings that can be found in places no one else thinks to look.

Nick and Katrina find that the garbage gods are with them in the Flea Market episodes.

- Nick and Katrina got down and dirty when they plunged into a dumpster to come up with a garment rack for Versacorp's wares in the Flea Market episode. "It's called being resourceful," Nick bragged. "Using things without paying for them." "Mr. Trump would be proud," agreed Katrina, still exhilarated from her first dumpster dive. "God, I want to look through some more garbage."

- Sandy stocked her Bridal Shop racks for next to nothing when she offered to take discontinued wedding dresses off salon owners' hands. "How many can you take?" enthused one shopkeeper, even as, elsewhere, opponent Chris R. struggled to get anyone to even take his call. Sandy wound up with plenty of inventory—and plenty of customers who liked the prices of the discontinued dresses.

This is where Brian's budget went during the Motel Hell challenge.

- Brian blundered unbelievably when he tore out sketchy toilets in the Motel Hell episode. Net Worth had a tremendous amount of work to do on the dilapidated motor inn they'd been ordered to improve. Rooms stank. Most everything had to go: carpets, beds, even ceiling tiles. Yet Brian busted his budget on bowls he didn't need. Although his teammates pointed out that a few new toilet seats would suffice, Brian refused to make do. He threw away what he could have recycled, and consequently, the team ran out of money before the job was done. Brian stuck Net Worth's funds where the sun don't shine, and, as Audrey pointed out in the series' most mug-worthy proverb, "Your ass doesn't know the difference."

"I took a big gamble on Joe Torre. Huge gamble. 'Clueless Joe,' that's what they called him because he'd been fired three or four places, see? But no one can make you feel inferior without your permission, that's what I tell my people. We took a risk because I had faith in him and I knew he could do it."

—George Steinbrenner

The "Packrat" sent Bren packing.

What's Life Without a Little Risk?

If Bren, the conservative lawyer from Tennessee, had trouble taking chances before signing on for *The Apprentice*, he must be positively gun-shy by now. His first leap of faith—coming up with the idea for the Dove Cool Moisture cucumber stroke—was a disaster. His last—helping Alex design the doomed Staples "Packrat"—was almost as bad. Yet it was Bren's aversion to risk that finally did him in. He and Alex were evenly matched in the Staples episode's boardroom until Bren confessed, "I definitely have trouble taking risks." It was then that Trump let him go. "He's a nice guy," observed the boss. "He's probably a good lawyer. He's not going to be an entrepreneur."

"Take risks, take chances, don't be afraid. You got to go into life brave."

—Billy Joel

"I don't like people who like to take foolish risks. But life is a risk . . . to be successful as an entrepreneur, you have to be a risk taker."

—Donald Trump

Wall Street legend and longtime Trump associate Alan "Ace" Greenberg oversaw Bear Stearns's growth into one of the world's most successful investment-banking firms.

"Don't overextend yourself, because leverage works in two directions. And usually when you're the most leveraged is when it goes down. And buy value. Don't listen to tips, nonsense, dreams. Buy stocks that earn money and you'll do fine."

—Alan "Ace" Greenberg's Investment Advice

Turn a No-Win into a Big Win

When Elizabeth felt Jennifer C. had set her up to fail in the Restaurant Opening task, she broke down and cried. John G. turned abusive when Audrey targeted him in the Miniature Golf episode. Chris R.'s body and spirits sank to the floor when Trump announced the Bridal Shop task. These candidates' emotions got the better of them in no-win situations. How might they have done better?

A Tale of Two Erins

Michael whined when he had to beat the drum for Magna's mobile spa in the Business on Wheels episode. He thought that selling massages to men was a no-win proposition. So he sulked while his teammates did all the work. Erin was incensed. "All Michael did is say 'I can't, I can't, I can't.' He should've turned the 'I can't' into 'How?' and 'I will!'" Which is exactly what Erin did. Rather than shrink from a street-hustling job for which she had no experience, she threw herself into it with gusto. "You will feel like the king that you are," she promised passersby "Real men get massages." Erin accurately summed up her performance when she said, "I was shameless and I got people in that door."

The fire in Erin's belly had gone out by the time Net Worth took on the Home Depot task. Her teammates rose to the challenge of putting on an in-store do-it-yourself clinic with a spirited, if inept, assembly of a mobile kitchen cabinet. Erin, on the other hand, stayed on the sidelines like the cheerleader she once was. Instead of "How?" and "I will!" the Business on Wheels way-shower said, "As a former beauty queen, I know what a crown is—but I don't know what crown molding is." This time around, Erin let the no-win get her down, so that's exactly where Trump sent her.

Erin was an enthusiastic spa saleswoman, but by the Home Depot task she was no longer level-headed.

Assert Yourself

Week after week, Andy resolved to combat his teammates' efforts to marginalize him. His youth and inexperience made him an easy scapegoat and he had to battle his way out of the boardroom three times in the first half of season two. "I felt like the kid in dodgeball who never gets picked," he admitted. A lesser competitor would've kept his head down after that. Instead, Andy emerged more determined than ever to make his mark. "I came here to win," he declared, "and that's what I plan on doing." He took charge in the NYPD Recruitment episode, put his rebellious older teammates in their places, and made good on his vow.

Rob went the other way in the Child's Play episode, clamming up after his Crustacean Nation idea—an eel with appendages—made teammates crabby. When The Donald asked why he'd gone into his shell, Rob said that project manager Pamela had underutilized him. Trump was skeptical. "A lot of people are underutilized because they don't choose to be utilized," he said. Rob didn't let his teammates know he was on board, so the train left without him.

"You've always got to stand up for yourself. You just have to fight for yourself, because basically nobody else is going to fight for you."

—Donald Trump

"I told the senior partner of Bear Stearns I was going to quit. And he said, 'Why?' and I said, 'Because you don't take [stock] losses and it just kills me to sit here and see these things disintegrate.' I met with him the next morning, and he said, 'Okay, anything you want to sell you have my permission to sell from here on.' So that morning I called over to the head of the order room and I started giving him sell orders and the whole room turned quiet. They thought the world was going to come to an end. And then the orders went down to the floor of the stock exchange and another senior partner who is a dear friend of mine said, 'Are you trying to get fired?' I said, 'Bill, it's okay, just go ahead and sell this s---.'"

—The Day "Ace" Greenberg had Enough

Distinguish Yourself on Day One

Pamela's one of the guys when she volunteers to lead them at season two's start.

When human beings are presented with information, they most easily remember the data that comes first. Psychologists call this the "Primacy Effect." This phenomenon applies to business, where first impressions tend to last. People size each other up within seconds and it's hard to get them to change their minds. You never get a second chance to make a first impression.

While season two's applicants mingled before their first task, Pamela and Bradford rose above the herd when they volunteered to lead the opposite sex's squad. Trump had just sorted the cast members by gender when he called for two brave souls to cross the lines. When others hesitated, Bradford knew he'd been given a chance to shine: "I mean, you have MBAs, Harvard grads, West Point men, and everyone's looking at each other, like, 'Who's gonna step up to the plate?'" Bradford and Pamela knocked Trump's first pitch over the wall—and the Primacy Effect ensured that everyone would remember who stepped forward when others held back.

Stacie J., on the other hand, made the worst kind of first-task impression when she consulted a Magic 8 Ball in front of her colleagues in the Child's Play episode. While Apex waited anxiously for Mattel to pick a winner in the task, Stacie asked the prophetic plaything for its prediction. When no one else cared what it said, Stacie flipped out. When her hysteria hushed the room, Stacie appeared to get paranoid. Her demands to know what was going on only isolated her further. Jennifer M. was "nervous." Sandy was "absolutely horrified." Ivana thought Stacie was "borderline schizophrenic." It was clear that when Apex had to throw someone to the wolves the choice would be nearly unanimous. An early meltdown had ensured a promising competitor's early exit. The Magic 8 Ball was wrong: Stacie's outlook was not good.

Stacie J. had a ball—until her teammates cringed.

Crunch Time Counts the Most

You can tell a lot about a person by the way he or she behaves when the heat is on. The greater the pressure, the more revealing the conduct. So viewers and prospective employers alike got a good look at the applicants' souls as the grueling *Apprentice* season wore on. Stress, strife, and sleeplessness eventually took their toll on everyone. Some, like Verna, gave up. Others, like Alex, got sloppy. A select few, like Kendra, only got better. When Trump chose her over Tana to be his third Apprentice, Kendra's excellence at "crunch time" was the reason. Tana had been the more assertive, creative, and energetic candidate for most of the season. But in those revealing final episodes, with the pressure cooker at its highest boil, Kendra came alive. The woman who'd once called a teammate an "ass" became the inspiring leader who could truthfully boast that her staff of misfits "worked harder for me than they ever did for themselves." Meanwhile, the fading Tana made big blunders—schlepping to Staten Island for a BeDazzler rather than planning her Hanes T-Shirt promotion; making New York's governor wait at the Athlete Challenge, then sending him onto the field without an American flag—which she then blamed on everyone but herself. Tana had gone into the home stretch looking like the favorite, but her crunch-time crumble told Trump more than she wanted him to know. He chose the finalist who glowed in the heat: Kendra.

Madeline Devries on Crisis Control

1) Be Prepared: Timing is everything in a crisis. The people who get that wrong just weren't prepared.

2) Be Honest. The more transparent you can be the better. Tell the truth and tell it quickly.

You have to go through drills with clients way before there's ever a crisis and usually if you do that there never is a crisis. It's almost like being trained to be an athlete. You can't run out and do a marathon and do well. You have to spend a lot of time mentally and physically preparing. Thinking through what can happen to you in the marketplace makes you smarter to make sure it doesn't happen.

"Get the big picture and get it fast. Concentrate on the solution, not just the problem. Ask yourself: Is this a catastrophe or is it a blip? That will help your equilibrium and your perspective."

—Donald Trump

CHAPTER 6
THE KEYS TO SUCCESSFUL SELLING

"Business is serving the needs and wants of other people. You don't succeed unless the others are happy. That forces you to pay attention to people. Even if you have a lousy personality that makes babies cry and you think you're just in it for yourself, if the customer isn't ultimately happy, then you fail." —Steve Forbes

Time and again, on *The Apprentice*, salesmanship made the difference between success and failure. All the meticulous preparations, the prestigious degrees, the impressive résumés, just didn't mean a thing if the customer didn't say "Yes." Or, worse, if there were no customers at all! Virtually every episode of *The Apprentice* was chock-full of lessons in how—and how not—to sell.

Tammy's ad walked the line and won the challenge for the women.

Net Worth's winning Nescafé event

"Substance" vs. "Sizzle"

- In season one's second episode, advertising legend Donnie Deutsch challenged the teams to come up with a multimedia ad campaign for Marquis Jet's private aircraft. The men of Versacorp, still smarting from the previous week's Lemonade Stand loss, took a sensible approach. They profiled their customer, selected images that showed how the product met his needs, and presented a glossy, professionally executed campaign. Nevertheless, the Protégé women walked away with another win. What did they have that the men didn't? In a word: balls. The women, following team member Tammy's titillating vision, had the audacity and the imagination to fill their jet photos with bold phallic imagery that made the men's slick work look generic. In the battle to attract eyeballs, Tammy's "testicle ad" was the clear winner. She'd heeded Donnie's advice to "swing for the fences," and scored a home run for Protégé.

"Don't be afraid to do it fresh, out of the box. Don't just do 'Oh, this is what an ad's supposed to look like.' The greatest advertising does it differently. The only thing I like to say to my people before I give them an assignment is, number one, swing for the fences, and failure is not an option. Just say to yourself, 'I'm winning this. Failure is not an option.'"

—Donnie Deutsch

- In season three, when Magna and Net Worth were ordered to put on a promotional event to hype Nescafé Taster's Choice, the Net Worth street smarts held a mock political debate in which rival "candidates" argued the merits of hot versus cold coffee drinks. Although there was also a $10,000 giveaway, the money seemed to attract less attention than the debaters' spirited exhortations and the free samples of Nescafé's product. Farther uptown, Magna kept its subdued event crowded by giving away iPods every half hour, but the coffee seemed like an afterthought. At the end of the day, Net Worth was the decisive winner—the result of coming up with more than just a giveaway: an event that may not have been smooth but definitely sizzled.

Aim for the Heart

- Donnie Deutsch knows that sometimes it takes more than facts and figures to do the job; for season two's NYPD Recruitment Campaign, he urged the teams to take an emotional approach, to find "what is going to motivate people to want to give of themselves—to serve—for their city." Then he added, "Don't screw up." Only one team met both conditions. Apex's ad evoked terrorism and promised a job on the front lines of the city's defense. Military hardware was a big selling point, and Raj in particular was like a kid in a candy store, raving, "We got millions of dollars of assets at our disposal!" While Apex produced its action film, Mosaic took a different tack. Project manager Andy rose to the occasion with a campaign that asked big questions—"When was the last time you saved a life?" "When was the last time you made your family proud?"—which in the television ad were posed by men and women of the NYPD, speaking directly into the camera. The spot felt intensely personal and aimed straight for the heart. When it came time to choose between a campaign that made hearts swell with pride and a campaign that made them quicken with fear, Donnie Deutsch didn't hesitate: Mosaic in a landslide.

There's too much hardware and not enough heart on display in Apex's war room.

Heart and Sold

Linda Sawyer discusses the roles of head and heart in the buying process—and how the best advertising speaks to both.

The way people approach buying is they start in a very rational place. Whether it's a really huge purchase like a home or a small purchase like hand soap, people develop a short list of the four or five things that are important to them and they go in with the intention of sticking to that list.

But then emotion kicks in. I use this example: every person who buys a house, they have usually very specific criteria—price, schools, a contemporary home— and then they walk into this house where things don't live up to the criteria but they happen to see this adorable little screened-in porch and little rocking chairs and all of a sudden they're fantasizing about sipping tea—which they will probably never have time to do anyway—and they convince themselves that they want this house.

So when we develop communications we merge the two: you have to responsibly give people information about the product and obviously you want to push those things that people desire in whatever the product or service is. You also want to leverage the strength of whatever this product or service is, and hopefully those two things converge. But then you need to really understand the insights of what motivates people, and you have to lens those benefits through those emotions. A lot of companies make the mistake of going in one direction or the other. Either clients say "All I want to do is sell, sell, sell and say it's the fastest, it's the best, it's the biggest selection, it's the lowest price"— that's never going to be enough. Some companies go completely the emotion route, and often that creates a desire but people feel unsatisfied because they don't have the information. So the best combination is when the two exist, and that makes for a very powerful communication.

Magna's all smiles when GM's executives love Kendra's "love affair with a car."

- Feelings can trump facts in more prosaic purchases, as Kendra proved in season three when she led Magna to victory in the Pontiac Solstice brochure episode. Tasked with the overnight production of a marketing booklet for Pontiac's sporty new two-seater, Kendra saw right away that it should highlight heat more than horsepower. "This is an emotional buy," she told her team. "Our brochure is going to tell the story of a love affair with a car." Kendra dispensed with details and instead filled her pages with feeling words like "desire" and photos that evoked those emotions. The job's GM judges were so enthusiastic about her final product that they decided to use it for the Solstice's U.S. release.

Meanwhile, the Net Worth men slunk into the boardroom after refusing to listen to their hearts. When Trump asked what they thought of the Solstice, all three applicants raved. "I love the car," gushed Chris S. "I'm gonna buy one." "Desire was the first word that came to me," said Bren, not realizing that he'd stumbled upon Kendra's triumphant approach too late. Carolyn made sure Net Worth got the message. "All three of you are talking about your emotions on this car," she pointed out. "You should have just put it in print." Instead of letting their feelings show, the men had stuck to the facts. The result was forgettable.

Asked what made Kendra and company the "slam dunk winner," the automotive execs said they'd "really nailed the emotion of the car."

Know Your Customer

It was hard not to wince when project manager Jason declared that a meeting with Marquis Jet executives to discuss their ad campaign would be "a waste of time." Even as he spoke, the Protégé women were plowing him under with knowledge gained from just such a meeting. In its second episode, *The Apprentice* had served up a lesson it would return to again and again: when it comes to meeting customers' needs, knowledge is power.

Hard Facts Beat the Hard Sell

The task in the Trump Ice episode was relatively straight-forward: sell as much of the stuff as possible. Sales whiz Nick decided he didn't need to do the online research that project manager Ereka wanted, and went to bed instead of doing his homework. The next day, however, Nick paid the price when he turned merchants off by appearing oblivious to their concerns. Luckily for the team, Bill jumped in with calculations that showed how much money could be saved by stocking Trump Ice instead of a competing brand. Nick turned up his nose at hitting the books, but the information therein proved much more alluring than his aggressive come-on.

No Butts About It: Mosaic's models stay sunny-side up rather than show off the parts that matter most to Levi's customers.

Hindsight Is 20/20

In the Levi's Catalogue episode, the teams competed to come up with the most appealing redesign of the Levi's Corporation's in-store catalogue. With a studio and a bevy of beautiful bony models at their disposal, team Mosaic pulled out every pose in the *Zoolander* playbook as they flooded each frame with skin and sin. Not once did somebody think to ask the obvious question: what do consumers look for in their jeans? Consequently, they wound up with virtually no butt shots, and a roomful of puzzled Levi's execs. Maria's explanation for the omission—that the jeans didn't fit right—only dug the hole deeper. Meanwhile, all Apex needed was a clear-eyed view of history to know that the key to victory was right in front of—better make that behind—them. They bypassed the models and put their own assets in front of the cameras. The jeans fit just right (and in Jennifer M.'s case made teammate Kelly widen his eyes and exclaim "Holy smokes! Cha cha!"), and Apex backed into a decisive victory.

Listen Up!

Tara had a clear vision for the mural she wanted in the Graffiti Billboard episode. Through direct communication and confident management, she made sure her team gave Sony PlayStation an ad that paid tribute to the surrounding Harlem neighborhood by acknowledging the "mean streets" found both there and in the new video-game release *Gran Turismo 4*. Unfortunately for Tara and her Net Worth team, however, it turned out there were no "mean streets" whatsoever in *Gran Turismo 4*. In fact, it appeared that Tara had decided on her vision before her meeting with PlayStation executives. So intent was she on realizing her concept that she seemed not to hear their instruction to appeal to hip urban 18–34-year-old males. She didn't even both-er to learn the game's contents. In contrast, decidedly unhip Alex simply walked across the street while his Magna team painted and asked some 18–34-year-old males what they thought. Alex listened—both to the client and to representatives of the demographic he needed to reach—and won.

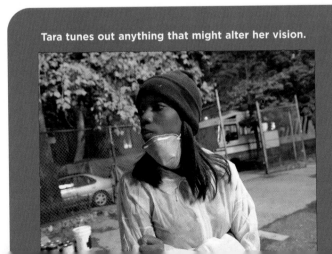

Tara tunes out anything that might alter her vision.

Find the Buyers Who Can Buy the Most and You Won't Have to Find the Most Buyers

When it comes to sales, sometimes quality is more important than quantity. Teams that sold indiscriminately rang up fewer wins than those that identified the most promising customers. As any major leaguer knows, pitch selection is more important than heat.

- Things looked grim for Magna in season three's Domino's Pizza episode when students swarmed the competition's Domino's Pizza truck outside the NYU dormitories. Net Worth project manager Stephanie seemed to have chosen the perfect location. Who, after all, eats more pizza than college students? But the comparative quiet around Magna's midtown location proved deceptive; Kendra and Tana had spent the previous day targeting local businesses, and their orders, though not as numerous, dwarfed those that Net Worth garnered from the street. The final tallies proved that Magna had out-grossed—and outsmarted—their rivals by selling in the right places.

- In season one, when Mr. Trump ordered Protégé and Versacorp down to the Trump Taj Mahal in Atlantic City, their mandate was to register gamblers through promotional events. The winner would be the team whose gamblers spent the most in the casino. Amy's team left no stone unturned in the effort to attract attention: they abused a bullhorn and hired showgirls to shepherd prospects their way. When the final tallies came in, it turned out that Amy had registered more gamblers by far. But it was Bill, with his laserlike focus on the recruitment of big-spending VIPs, who hit the jackpot and handed Amy her worst loss of the season. Though fewer in number, the VIPs had outspent Amy's gamblers by a mile.

Determination and decolletage drew more gamblers to Amy's table, but Bill's big-spending VIPs proved the better bet.

Know How to Reach Your Customer

Okay, your marketing sizzles and you know precisely who your customer is. Now you have to introduce the two, or you'll end up like Katrina in the Apartment Renovation episode: twiddling your thumbs in an apartment you just whipped into shape while the world passes you by. Katrina had overseen a first-rate renovation and seemed well on her way to winning the task of increasing rent by the highest percentage. But her inability to get the word out left Versacorp at the mercy of their sole prospective tenant. The single offer can be a salesperson's nightmare, and Katrina, a successful realtor, should have known it. Just one more bidder might have made the difference between victory and the boardroom.

- In season two's Bridal Shop episode, the teams fought for a piece of the bridal biz, soliciting vendors and decorating spaces for big blowout one-day sales. But the task would be won or lost in the battle for brides, and only one team figured out how to reach them. Mosaic fired off an e-mail blast to 23,000 brides and drew customers in droves, while Apex haplessly tried to drum up business at Manhattan's commuter rail stations—not, as Trump pointed out, the places most conducive to matrimonial dreams.

> *"Be truthful. There's nothing wrong with saying, 'I don't think that's the best dress for you,' but you have to have another suggestion. You don't just say, 'Well, see you.'"*
> —Bridal salon owner Bernadette, on matching customer with product

Versacorp can't drag a soul up to their freshly renovated apartment.

Ivana can't catch commuters' eyes during Apex's misdirected marketing push.

Madeline DeVries on the Well-Aimed Blast

E-mail blasts are great, but one has to be thoughtful about marketing. The whole point of marketing is to sell a product. If I e-mail you and annoy you, you're not buying my product. Buzz which connects consumers to brands is fabulous. When you're just doing it to do it, it's a waste of time.

Sightseers get more than they bargained for when Troy takes the mic atop a tourist bus.

Don't Walk Away Once the Customer's in the Door

- In season one, outside Planet Hollywood, three Versacorp men clowned, pleaded, and even hijacked a bus in order to attract customers. Determined to increase the evening's sales by a higher percentage than the Apex women, they mustered an effort that was heroic—and misplaced. With so much manpower out front, no one was available to guide customers to the right place once they were inside. Diners breezed right by the high-margin sales locations, such as the merchandise counter and the bar.

  When the women took over Planet Hollywood, the real work began once the customer crossed the threshold. They maintained a dynamic presence at the point of purchase to pump up alcohol sales (where Kristi knew restaurants make their largest chunk of profit), and make the most of the evening's traffic. Customers—particularly the male ones— spent freely in the partylike atmosphere. The Apex women won big with a personal selling approach.

- In season three's Burger King episode, the teams were asked to take over individual franchises and, while running every station in the restaurant themselves, launch a new sandwich with as much fanfare as possible. After Net Worth handed Magna a solid drubbing, self-described marketing maven Danny boasted in the boardroom that he'd sent a lot of people through the door. Carolyn wasn't impressed. "The objective was not to get them in," she said, noting that once inside the customers ignored the team's new sandwich. Team Magna failed to realize that the task wasn't in the bag until their product was.

Know Your Product

The Art Gallery episode highlighted something every salesperson should know: ignorance is not bliss. Striving to outsell the other team during rival gallery shows, Mosaic project manager Nick overrode his teammates' objections and chose to showcase the work of the accessible artist Andrei. By his own admission, Nick was no canvas connoisseur, so on what did he base his decision? He knew that he'd be able to sell Andrei's art because he understood it.

In contrast, Kwame's Versacorp team overrode their own qualms about Meghan's esoteric and disturbing artwork when they learned about the high price tags and established fan base that came with it. But when it came time to sell, Versacorp was a comedy of errors. No one was qualified to answer questions about Meghan's work. No one even really liked it. Troy and Heidi tried to pretend they were knowledgeable about art, and both wound up embarrassing themselves in front of customers who actually did. "I messed up on some pictures," Heidi admitted after calamitously misidentifying a fireplace cover. "But hell, that looked like a damn toilet seat if I ever saw one." The evening's one success happened when Omarosa was smart enough to call Meghan over to explain the work herself. When someone who knew the product got involved, the team finally made a sale.

> *"You've got to believe in what you're selling. If you don't really believe it yourself, it'll never work. It'll never sell, and you're going to be miserable."*
>
> – Donald Trump

A copier salesman knows a true original when he sees it; Nick chooses the artist he understands.

Heidi clearly doesn't understand her team's artist's work; she identifies one piece as a toilet seat.

The M&M Sisters prove that style trumps sex in the M-Azing Bar episode.

"In-house, we call our total experience here the Trump Experience. And it starts with a member or a guest being greeted properly right through the entire day: the golf course is in perfect condition, the staff members are the top quality staff. It's not so much about the product: the product goes with the service. The goal here is to make everything top-notch."

—Carolyn Kepcher

Sell The Experience

Question: would you rather pay $5 or $2 for the exact same chocolate bar? Don't jump to conclusions: In season two's M-Azing Bar episode—in which teams peddled treats they'd made themselves in the M&M/Mars factory—more New Yorkers opted for the higher price. Why? For $5 they got to meet the ravishing M&M Sisters, better known as Sandy and Jennifer M. with their matching outfits, identical hairstyles, and gigantic smiles. A block away, the lackluster salesmanship of Ivana, Kelly, and Kevin failed to stimulate passersby, even at less than half the M&M Sisters' price.

Likewise, $5 is a ripoff for a cup of lemonade . . . unless Kristi's phone number happens to be on the napkin, as it may have been during the Protégé women's season one Lemonade Stand victory. In both instances, none of the customers who swarmed to these saleswomen thought they got a raw deal. They paid for an experience, not just for a product, and seemed more satisfied than the people who purchased identical refreshments from the losing team at a fraction of the price.

"I wouldn't pay five dollars for a glass of lemonade, but if it was served by a very pretty girl—you might be surprised. I might pay a dollar for the lemonade, four dollars for the girl."

—George Ross

Have Fun!

Well, sure, it's easy to love what you do when you're doing it in your own private jet. But you don't have to get to the top to have fun—it's the other way around. In order to make their fortunes take flight, the *Apprentice* applicants had to learn the simple value of a smile.

- Troy was as low as he could go: charged with making the most money in a day as the head of a Pedicab Fleet in season one, he watched helplessly while his vehicles sat empty at the curb, his marketing brainstorm—prepaid ride cards—proved as popular with New Yorkers as the Red Sox, and the other team's pedicabs rolled by covered with advertising that he'd never thought to sell. But rather than throw up his hands, Troy threw on his hat, grabbed some handlebars, and took to the streets as the free-wheelin' Rickshaw Cowboy. All at once, sales turned the corner.

- Andy practically had his thumb in the soup as he bobbled plates and mixed up orders after being conscripted as a bus-boy in the Restaurant Opening episode in season two. Because service, as rated by the Zagat's guide, counted for a full third of the team's final score, Andy's gaffes could have cost Mosaic dearly. Thanks to his irrepressible cheer, however, patrons only smiled. Meanwhile, across town the Apex women's surly faces and project manager Jennifer C.'s thinly veiled disdain for her clientele got them blasted in Zagat's as "too many women in black milling around like a bunch of uptight stewardesses." The women didn't have a good time, so neither did their customers.

"If you don't love what you're doing . . . forget it. Do something else. You'll be much more successful and you'll lead a much happier life."

—Donald Trump

One of Versacorp's pedicab ads

Troy takes to the streets as the Rickshaw Cowboy.

No one seemed to be having any fun at Apex's Restaurant opening.

- Red Velvet Ice Cream's coming-out party ought to have been a blast in season two's Ciao Bella episode, but the mood was somber around the Apex cart. The women didn't seem willing to roll up their sleeves and sell. Project manager Ivana insisted "I'd rather lose than sell sex." But was that really the issue? Across Times Square, the bow-tie–bedecked men showed how spirit translates into sales. If fun is contagious, the sidewalk around the Donut Ice Cream cart was the center of an epidemic. Passersby were happy to join the party—one even took a turn with the scoop—while the women's restrained approach made it easy for speedwalking New Yorkers to blow right by.

To Thy Brand Be True

"Fun is a good thing. People like to be entertained, people like to be amused, people love to laugh, so obviously if you can inject that appropriately it's always a good thing. The one caution I would give is that it has to be appropriate for what you're selling. There are some things that are serious and the tone needs to be consistent so fun would be inappropriate and distasteful and offensive. So you have to be careful. I also think fun can't be for the sake of getting attention, it has to be appropriate and a shared value of the brand that you're selling."

— Linda Sawyer

"I find that the more you enjoy your job the more successful you are at it."

— Carolyn Kepcher

A white tiger is Protégé's coup de grâce during season one's Casino episode.

Selling with Spectacle: Bigger Is Better

The Donald knows that to make a splash it's better to cannon-ball off the high dive than to step cautiously into the shallow end. His Taj Mahal was built to accommodate the largest gambling floor in the world; his development on Manhattan's West Side originally included plans for the world's tallest building. Applicants who weren't afraid to think big often won their tasks—and The Donald's nod of approval.

- It took a lot to attract gamblers' attention amid the Taj Mahal's bustle, but Bill's Protégé team got it done with a giant $1,000 giveaway roulette wheel—ushered in with a trained tiger. The team's promotional event looked right at home in a place where extravagance is the norm. On the other hand, Versacorp's $300 car rental looked decidedly puny. Amy got a rare scolding from Trump, who noted that at the Taj you don't give away a rental, you give away the whole car.

A compact car rental isn't big enough for Trump's taste.

"When I built Trump Tower I said I wanted to build the greatest building in the world, and I also wanted it to be a huge attraction to draw people in and spend lots of money. So what I did is I constructed a waterfall that's six stories tall that's gotten the best architectural reviews probably of anything I've done. People come from all over the world to visit Trump Tower and to see the waterfall. And all of the shops and restaurants benefit."

—Donald Trump

- In season three's Burger King episode, Net Worth's Tana and Kristen braved a broker's dingy apartment and incontinent pooch to retrieve a pair of airline tickets to Las Vegas for their promotion's grand prize. A trip to Sin City was an attractive lure compared with the scene outside the rival Magna franchise, where Danny's "Triple Play" ball toss looked like it had been built out of trash from the restaurant's dumpster. "It looks like a bunch of drunk hippies threw some stuff together to make a little raft to float on," complained Alex as customers veered to avoid the promotion. "Danny is a steamroller with a drunk driver at the helm." Carolyn could only shake her head. "This is sad," she said. "This is very sad." While seeking to sell with spectacle, Danny had instead made a spectacle of himself.

"There's a difference between selling sex and selling sex. You can look good, you can have a proper uniform on, and you can kick their ass."

—Donald Trump

Heidi and Katrina boogie for bullion.

Sex Sells . . . But Don't Go Too Far

In season one, sex was in the boardroom, on the street, and in the suite; it affected negotiations and divided teammates. Good for ratings, sure, but was it good for business? Early on, the answer seemed to be yes, as sex appeal helped the women of Protégé trounce the men four times in a row. At the end of that run, however, they found themselves unexpectedly called on the carpet by Trump and Carolyn, who felt that the skin-and-win strategy had gone too far. "You beat the guys fair and square," said The Donald. "But you're coming a little close to crossing the line, relying on your sexuality to win." So where is that line, and how can the savvy salesperson sex it up without crossing it?

Tummy Time: Trump and Carolyn marveled when Kristi revealed her marvelous abs on the job.

Sex Is Not a Substitute

Donald Trump is a master of the art of negotiation, and you can be sure that his toolkit does not include the virtual pole dance that Heidi and Katrina performed to win a discount on a gold bar in season one's Buying Low episode. Successful though it was, their performance was better suited to a bachelor party than to a place of business. The same could be said for Amy's ploy to win a break on ten pounds of squid: "Kristi, would you show him your stomach?" These were the sort of skills that Carolyn referred to when she advised "Things like that aren't going to get you the job here."

"They actually had to say to us 'Too much sex,' and that's embarrassing."
— Kristi

Katrina bats her perfect lashes even after Carolyn's tongue lashing.

Beware the Spillover Effect

Katrina was quite the coquette when it suited her; in the Casino episode she went into the negotiation for the free car rental with no plan other than a gorgeous smile. Team leader Amy fumed that "Katrina has a tendency to use sexuality as her prime negotiating tactic." So it was hard to take Katrina seriously in the Pedicab Fleet episode when she huffed that Bill wanted to exploit her good looks to sell fares. "What about my ideas? I'm not a pinup doll," she complained. But if Katrina wanted to be valued for her brain, then using it should have been her prime negotiating tactic.

"If being attractive is wrong, then we did something wrong."
— Amy

"It's a fine line. The experience must be something which is pleasant and not totally disturbing or unusual. So, buying lemonade from a pretty woman to me is okay. On the other hand, buying a candy bar from someone who says 'I'll drop my skirt if you buy the candy bar' is a different ball game. In the first one, they pass the lemonade, there's nothing that went with it except she handed you the lemonade and said five dollars. It wasn't a quid pro quo."

— George Ross

It's All About the Product

M-Azing Error: Ivana puts the wrong mouth-watering wares on display.

Pants on Fire: Maria burns out with a misdirected Levi's campaign.

Exhibit A: Ivana's butt. When she showed it to a roomful of executives in the Levi's Catalogue episode, no one batted an eye, sex appeal and their product go hand in hand. When she dropped her skirt to sell a $20 chocolate bar, she went way out of bounds; sex and that product don't usually go together except in fetish films. Carolyn cut to the chase when she said, "You weren't selling a candy bar." Sex should lead to the product, not vice versa.

Exhibit B: Maria's modeling meltdown in season two. Maria's frazzled orchestration of the Levi's Catalogue modeling shoot made her—and project manager Wes—look pretty bad, but in the end the models looked pretty good. After Mosaic's presentation to Levi's executives, President Robert Hanson gave the team credit for bringing a sexy pitch, but noted that they'd neglected to bring the product. Maria had orchestrated a steamy photo shoot that showed off the models, not the pants.

Know When to Shoot for the Moon on Price

Knowing what to say when the customer asks "how much?" is a crucial talent for any salesperson. *The Apprentice* offers lessons in how to find the magic number.

- In season one's Penthouse Rental episode, the teams competed to lease the spectacular space at the top of Trump World Tower for the greatest sum. Bill, Kwame, and Troy did their homework and opened negotiations with interested customers at a figure that matched what the space had fetched in the past. But they'd underestimated the appeal of "Trump luxury." On the other team, Nick threw out the rule book and named an outrageously high figure. He knew that he was offering a totally unique product that could not easily be compared to any other; the customer's desire would determine its value. Nick got his price, and a trip to Mar-a-Lago with Amy, while Bill, Kwame, and Troy packed their bags for the boardroom.

- In the QVC TV episode, Pamela ordered Stacy to set the price for the blocks of cleaning pads that the team planned to sell on the air. When Stacy equivocated, Pamela took over and came up with a figure herself. Brushing aside teammates' concerns about overpricing, she shot for the moon. Unlike Nick, however, Pamela wasn't selling "Trump luxury." She was selling an everyday item in a marketplace full of alternatives. It was a costly blunder. QVC viewers stayed away from their phones, and Apex's sluggish sales sent Pamela to the street.

- You didn't need a business degree to know that Mosaic was in trouble when Wes and Kevin set prices for the clothing in their Fashion Show by simply doubling designer Ilsa's figures. All episode long it was obvious that the men were, as Carolyn put it, "clearly out of their element;" they'd literally reduced her to tears of laughter with their zombielike wanderings through a fabric warehouse. Nevertheless, Wes and Kevin made no effort to educate themselves about the fashion industry, no effort to determine what the market would make of their figures. They were way out of line, and their miscalculation made fashion victims of Mosaic.

Carolyn cracks up when the men turn fashion victims.

Push comes to shove when Troy's pushiness makes bidders shove off.

Sometimes It's a Mistake to Do the Hustle

A second bidder is the salesperson's greatest boon. Troy appeared to be sitting pretty when a new customer materialized just as he was about to close a deal for the Penthouse Rental. But Troy squandered the opportunity when he pushed too hard too fast to ignite a bidding war. The new arrival felt that he was being hustled and withdrew his offer. If Troy had instead found a way to soothe the bidder's jitters, he might not have been bounced from the boardroom the next day.

Balance Your Focus

- The teams started the M-Azing Bar episode on the M&M/Mars factory floor where they handcrafted the next day's wares. When Ivana, Kevin, and Kelly churned out more bars, it looked as if they had Sandy and Jennifer M. licked. But while Ivana's team worked efficiently on the factory floor, they neglected to plan the next day's marketing strategy. The oversight cost Ivana dearly when the competition overtook her with well-executed salesmanship and a pair of short denim skirts.

- Likewise, in the Bridal Shop episode, Chris R. agonized over the presence of industry veteran Sandy on the other team and tried to compensate by bringing in lots of inventory and persuading a salon owner to help set up their store. Chris wound up with a good-looking shop, but so much time and energy devoted to inventory and its presentation meant there wasn't much left for marketing. Meanwhile, rival project manager Kelly's first act was to split Mosaic into procurement and marketing divisions. Result: Kelly's shop opened to a line of more than forty customers, while Chris's opened to two.

Coal In The Stocking: Apex frets over stocking their shop rather than make a marketing plan.

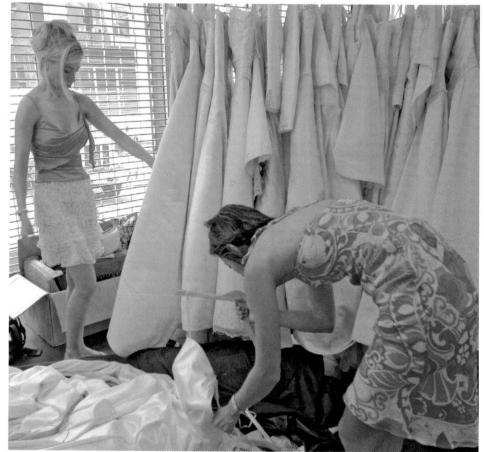

Run, run, as fast as you can—you're still not going to attract customers to your lemonade stand.

Not All Salespeople Are Created Equal

Nick bragged that telling him how to sell was "like trying to tell the Pope how to pray." Chris R. was smooth enough to win diners' raves even while privately admitting, "I hate the public, bro." Ivana—a cool customer behind the scenes, during presentations, and in the boardroom—unraveled whenever it was time to sell on the street. Pamela's public face was icier than her Donut Ice Cream in Times Square, and a hyperactive David frightened customers away from Versacorp's lemonade stand by running after them with a sign.

When it comes to person-to-person sales, we are not all equally blessed. Be honest with yourself. Are you a numbers-oriented Bill or a charmingly crass Chris? An in-your-face Nick or a catch-more-flies-with-honey Katrina? Do you sell more effectively with facts or with feelings? Or, like Jennifer C., should you have a restraining order keeping you fifty feet from the point of sale? *The Apprentice* applicants who succeeded were realistic about their strengths and weaknesses and tailored their strategies accordingly.

CHAPTER 7

MANAGEMENT TALES FROM THE FRONT

*"Expect people to do their best. Be their example. Give them chances.
Offer a challenge. The best people will respond with their best, and those
are the people you want around. It's a simple formula, and it works."*
—Donald Trump

Every *Apprentice* applicant came to the boardroom table already a winner. They varied in degree of success, but each and every one of them was a standout: intelligent, confident, ambitious, successful in their field. Why, then, did they so often stumble? And why did their mistakes seem so terribly obvious? Not that anyone's complaining—we all enjoyed feeling superior to self-professed masters of the universe when they blundered (even though it's unlikely we would have fared any better). Still, it came as a shock to see how many of them were thrown off their games by the show's team-oriented format. Project managers had to figure out how to take groups of highly individualistic cast mates with varied skill sets, temperaments, and egos, and make them productive. The results were usually entertaining but not very good business. Clearly there's a world of difference between having talent and managing it. Along with hard lessons in humility, applicants learned sound strategies for getting the most out of a team.

> *"To build confidence in the people who work for you, don't make yourself too important. If you start putting all the [attention] on yourself, that's not right. You've got to be willing to put it on the people that are around you."*
>
> —George Steinbrenner

Pamela's stature keeps Raj on his toes . . .

. . . and her iron fist keeps the Apex women on theirs.

Raj decides that being "stifled" by Jennifer M. might not be such a bad thing.

How to Take Charge of a New Team

After three consecutive losses, Apex was in a tailspin. Season two had barely begun, and already the women were squabbling and backbiting with abandon. Turning them around in the QVC TV episode would be a gigantic task, and Mr. Trump knew just the woman for the job.

Pamela was up to that point perhaps first among equals, tough enough to stand tall with the men (literally: "It's intimidating for me, by the way, to talk to a woman who's substantially taller than me," confessed Raj. Pamela retorted, "Get used to that feeling"), and savvy enough to win the approval of fellow Wharton School alumnus Donald J. Trump, who publicly declared his respect as he handed over Apex's reigns. True to form, Pamela rolled into her new team like a Sherman tank. "I don't know the personalities," she announced. "I don't know what's happened in the past. Here's what I want you to know: I don't [bleep]ing care!"

She should have cared. When Trump demanded to know, after yet another Apex defeat, how Pamela had evaluated her team's abilities, all she could say was, "I asked." Trump pounced. "You have to assess them yourself," he said. As Pamela took the elevator to the street, he noted. "She's so opinionated, and she's so sure of herself, and everything she says seems to be wrong." Pamela's hard-nosed style led to a shockingly early exit for a woman who many thought might go all the way.

The Doggie Business episode showcased two inclusive leadership styles that might have served Pamela well. After a team-scrambling "corporate shuffle" put Wes and Jennifer M. in charge of unfamiliar faces, each took the time to make informed judgments about their newcomers' assets. For example, Wes sat down with Stacy R. and communicated his impression of her, then invited her to fill in the blanks. Their give-and-take let Wes uncover skills he might have overlooked, and confirm existing suspicions (such as the fact that Stacy asks too many questions). Meanwhile, Jennifer spoke with her new arrivals as a group and had them describe one another's strengths and weaknesses. By keeping the mood light, she built camaraderie even as these peer-performance reviews told her what she needed to know. For instance, when Kevin, while praising Raj's creativity, called him "long-winded," Jennifer laughed and promised, "I'll be here to stifle you." A relaxed and respectful atmosphere had enabled both Jennifer and Raj to learn from Kevin's feedback.

In exchange for letting teammates know that their opinions mattered, Wes and Jennifer received the benefit of their experience—and their loyalty. Unlike Pamela, they went into the task with their teams united behind, not against, them.

"Success breeds success."
—Donald Trump

Nick is pleased with his team's efforts in the Flea Market episode.

Look at the Record

No matter whose example you follow when evaluating your team, don't rely on words alone; as they say in politics, "Look at the record." Nick became the first male project manager to score a win in season one by following this good advice. After Trump gave him a chance in the Flea Market episode to poach talent from the ranks of the undefeated all-female Protégé, Nick took a look at his recruits' win/loss record and made the wisest possible choice: he got out of their way. "They've won four in a row," he observed. "Obviously they're doing something right." Nick watched bemusedly as Versacorp's new faces chose, tailored, and sold the product with more success than the team had ever seen. At the end of the day, Versacorp's surviving members had learned how to win. Nick didn't make many strong choices, but he made the one that counted: he trusted the record.

Know Your Staff's Strengths and Weaknesses, and Play to Them

Jennifer M. said of Raj, "He sees the strengths and weaknesses of the other team members and that's critical to being a good leader," by which she meant he didn't like Ivana either. But she had nevertheless made a good point. The superior applicants knew how to read people. But some, like Raj, didn't always let that knowledge guide their decisions when the time came to lead. The best project managers always matched the right person with the right job.

Omarosa and her teammates put personal feelings aside during the Marquis Jet presentation.

Queen of Comedy: Kristen lightens up during the Dove Cool Moisture task.

- It's hard to imagine a more combative trio than season one's Heidi, Ereka, and Omarosa. Ereka and Omarosa goaded one another like boxers at a weigh-in, and lunchtime with Heidi and Omarosa meant more bleeps than an episode of *The Osbournes*. Yet, in the Marquis Jet episode, Amy's deft management steered this wild bunch to victory with nary a hiccup. How'd she do it? First, rather than waste time trying to get Ereka and Omarosa to play nice, she separated them; unable to get in her adversary's face, each woman focused on the job. Later, when it came time to plan Protégé's pitch to Donnie Deutsch, Amy didn't let Omarosa and Heidi's personal friction keep her from capitalizing on their strong presentation skills. Careful definition of each woman's role enabled Amy to put them right out front, and they rewarded her confidence with compelling performances and flawless teamwork. Whatever battles awaited them back in the suite, Protégé's fiery-tempered women excelled when it mattered. Amy's smart management kept turmoil to a minimum, and the team's winning streak alive.

- Kwame took the opposite tack in the Art Gallery episode, sending Heidi and Omarosa out unsupervised to work with the artist while he and Troy handled invitations. It's natural that Kwame would prefer his friend Troy's company, but given that Heidi was by now calling Omarosa "an absolute lunatic bitch" and Omarosa was insisting that Heidi "clean up her act and shut her mouth," trouble was all but guaranteed. Kwame's decision to turn a blind eye to his teammates' weaknesses helped set Heidi and Omarosa at each other's throats.

- In the Dove Cool Moisture episode, Net Worth's project manager, Kristen, proved that being a director's girlfriend doesn't exactly make you the next Scorcese. After embracing John and Craig's idea for a comedic ad about a marathon runner refreshing himself with body wash, Kristen promptly sent both men away from the set. The absence of those two strong competitors made it easier for her to bully everyone around the soundstage, but she'd left herself at the helm of an advertising *Ishtar*. No one had any idea how to deliver a joke. Kristen seemed uncertain whether it even was a joke, later insisting, "I was never going for funny." The last laugh belonged to Magna, whose members survived their own awful effort thanks only to Kristen's refusal to play to her staff's strengths.

The Case for Dictatorship

Let staff members know that you value their opinions, but don't forget that the objective is to formulate your own. This lesson became clear as numerous teams fell apart under mob rule. Leaders who let their followers call the shots rarely made it out of the boardroom.

- Project manager Kristi refused to make an executive decision about what Protégé should sell at the flea market. "I don't want to be a dictator," she said while her crew scoured Manhattan's shops. "I want to make sure the team's on board, too." Unfortunately for Kristi, the team was waiting for her to act like, well, a leader. It was 7 P.M. before Kristi made her tentative choice. Protégé left Chinatown loaded with hats, umbrellas, and doubts about their project manager's performance under pressure. "I tried to lead by group consensus," Kristi confessed in the boardroom. "That was one of my biggest mistakes."

> *"Managing people, it's always easier to loosen up rather than tighten up."*
>
> —George Steinbrenner

- Lobster ice cream. Bloody Mary. Old Bay sorbet. Project manager Ivana was willing to entertain any idea for a new Ciao Bella flavor. After squirming under Bradford's bullying leadership during the previous task, she was determined to let each and every team member have a say. Sure enough, the deadline for flavor selection loomed and Apex was in disarray. Privately, Bradford expressed his sense of vindication: "It may be too much of the velvet glove and not enough iron fist." Only Maria's last-minute suggestion, Red Velvet Ice Cream, spared New York from experiencing a frozen treat that contained crustaceans. Ivana had learned a tough lesson: cast too wide a net and you'll reel in a lot of junk.

> *"Ultimately, lack of organization is lack of leadership, and you cannot succeed with a lack of leadership."*
>
> —Donald Trump

Just a few of Apex's rejected ice-cream flavor ideas

Cranb. scones
Fried Twinkl
Buttermilk biscuit
Taramisu
Fried Chicken
Bachlava
Peppers
Citron tunic
Lichees
Licor

- Sometimes a conversion from dictatorship to democracy can be nothing but a leader's effort to keep his head safe from the chopping block. This appeared to be the case in the Nescafé Taster's Choice episode when Danny called for a vote on whether or not to hire an event planner for Magna's marketing extravaganza. The price was high and the team had no marketing strategy, but time was running out. Clearly, whoever made such an important decision would be vulnerable in the boardroom should it turn out badly. So Danny dithered, morale plummeted, and Michael balanced plates on his head. Ironically, Danny's effort to escape blame is what, in the end, ensured that he'd take it all.

Amy tries to keep her cool in the Trump Ice episode.

"Surround yourself with smart people. People smarter than you are. That's very important. Don't ever be afraid of talent."
—George Steinbrenner

Know Your Role

Pairing salespersons with complementary styles can work wonders; charmers like Katrina and Ereka often opened doors for no-nonsense negotiators like Amy and Bill through sheer charisma. But things break down when partners don't respect each other's roles.

For example, Heidi knew just whom to pair with even-tempered Amy in the Trump Ice episode. "I put Omarosa and Amy together because I knew that, honestly, Amy could deal with Omarosa," she explained. At first Heidi's instinct proved correct as Omarosa's smooth marketing pitches set Amy up perfectly to close the sales. But Omarosa couldn't seem to leave the limelight. As Amy looked on in disbelief, she sold tiny amounts of water to customers who might have bought more. Soon Amy was kicking her partner underneath the table in a futile effort to shut her up. The duo finished the day with just pocket change and a bruised shin, evidence that line-crossing has its price.

Don't Fear Talent

The Apprentice's strongest leaders didn't hesitate to surround themselves with the best possible people. In season one, Nick's final-four finish was in no small part due to this practice. A copier salesman who could without irony declare himself Donald Trump's kindred spirit wasn't one to shy away from rival talents—or egos. "I have assembled a phenomenal team," Nick boasted in the Flea Market episode, and he had: Amy, Bill, Katrina, and Ereka. Given the chance by Trump to select teammates like a grade-school captain in gym class, Nick bested Kristi pick for pick. During his next outing as project manager,

in the Art Gallery episode, Nick proved his mettle once again by nabbing Amy back from Protégé when The Donald offered him the pick of the litter. Being brave enough to stand with the brightest stars proved that Nick was one of them.

In contrast, Wes unloaded his star player, Kelly, when Trump told him to send one person over to Apex at the beginning of the Levi's Catalogue task. Wes claimed that he couldn't afford to lose anyone else's skill set, but Kelly wasn't fooled: "He pushed me away . . . because I'm stronger than he is." Mr. Trump seemed inclined to agree. "You have a very good man," he said as Apex celebrated their new arrival. Wes's choice demoralized his team and bolstered the competition's strength, but the real damage was to his credibility as a manager. Sensing weakness at the top, the team ran wild: Maria took over the photo shoot, long heated quarrels ate up precious minutes, and even Wes's allies marveled privately at his failure to exercise leadership. Mosaic's loss wasn't surprising, and Wes had inadvertently sealed it before the task even began.

Nip Quarrels in the Bud

Early intervention saved Kelly's hide when his team began to unravel during preparations for the Genworth/Trump Polo Cup in season two's finale. The trouble began when Raj and John W. defied Elizabeth's order to move a sponsor's broken sign and instead commandeered a golf cart for a joyride around the grounds. Proving that even the most mild-mannered applicant has her breaking point, Elizabeth leaped into another golf cart and took off in hot pursuit. *The Apprentice*'s first-ever chase scene made its way back to Kelly, where the combatants squared off. Elizabeth, showing verve that would have served her well during the NYPD Recruitment task, proclaimed herself "Dictator Elizabeth," prompting Raj to question her authority. It could have been the end of the line for Kelly in his pursuit of the Apprenticeship. Instead, he deployed skills that helped define him as the ultimate winner.

**Raj and John flee from
Elizabeth's demands.**

Get the Facts

Kelly made sure he understood the nature of the conflict before trying to resolve it. Rather than shut down his squabbling staffers, he listened until he'd learned their points of view. No one walked away frustrated that they hadn't been heard. Neither did they get the chance to waste the day with their complaints: as soon as Kelly had the facts, he moved on.

Make a Clear Decision

Kelly solved both immediate and future dustups by expressing himself in no uncertain terms. He reminded his staffers of their distinct responsibilities, and insisted that they defer to each other in their respective departments. He also forcefully emphasized the value of consideration and cooperation with a deadline looming. Kelly's assertiveness was a smokejumper's fire set in the path of a runaway blaze; it extinguished a potentially catastrophic problem. Even Raj, no Kelly fan, walked away impressed with his manager's mediation skills. The team emerged from a potential crisis more than ever focused on success.

Know When to Delegate

You Can't Do It Alone

Raj and John W.'s golf cart goof-off happened in part because Kelly underutilized them. Sure, there was little love lost between the fired applicants and their boss, but the team's competitive natures at first kept them focused. "I'm doing this because I like winning," said Raj as the van left for the Polo Cup, adding, "I couldn't give a damn about Kelly." Attention drifted, however, as Kelly delegated only mindless tasks like stuffing gift bags and placing signs. Important jobs, to be sure, but Raj and John wanted to know that they were valued as more than grunt labor. When Kelly later demanded that staff members exercise autonomy within their departments, spirits soared and the team cruised through the rest of the day. A little responsibility elicited a much bigger investment in the project. If Kelly had involved everyone in planning right from the start, he would have sent a respectful message and avoided much of the day's trouble.

Avoid an Energy Crisis

The Restaurant Opening task was a monumental challenge in a short amount of time. Apex and Mosaic had to transform dingy vacant establishments into inviting eateries overnight. Both teams wore themselves out planning menus, decor, and marketing. At 4 A.M. the exhausted Apex women were still mopping and scrubbing. When they finally stumbled back to the suite for an hour or two of rest, they found the competition snug in their beds. Project manager Raj had hired cleaners to do the dirty work while the Mosaic men enjoyed a good night's sleep! The next day, diners enjoyed service with a smile from Mosaic's refreshed staff. Over at Apex, the women's black dresses suited an atmosphere that was as dreary as a wake. It was, in fact, Jennifer C.'s professional funeral, as her failure to subcontract the cleaning job helped to land her in a yellow cab at the episode's end. Working smarter doesn't always mean working longer—when it comes to energy, make sure you spend it all in the right place.

The women spend all night cleaning their restaurant . . .

. . . but it's the men who look freshly scrubbed the next day, thanks to a good night's sleep.

Know Your Place

Stephanie dug her own grave in the Domino's Pizza episode's boardroom as she seized every possible opportunity to recall the Domino's Pizza delivery to Brooklyn that supposedly explained her absence from the team's Manhattan truck. Ignoring George's increasingly puzzled expression, she blamed Alex and Chris for taking the far-flung order, and insisted that her 90-minute trek demonstrated her commitment to corporate honor. When Stephanie finally stopped shoveling, George asked the obvious: "Why couldn't you delegate that?" Given that Stephanie's hired herd of promotional models had spent the day milling aimlessly about, the question was a killer. Trump said as much when he sent Stephanie packing: "A good leader would've stayed with her team where she was needed most."

"If you pick the right person, you're a hero. If you pick the wrong person, you're a bum. It's as simple as that. I also think you have to have the ability to make the decision, and to make it stick. And may God have mercy that you made the right one."

—George Ross on Delegation

Delegation Is Not Abandonment

Assigning responsibility is not the same thing as dodging it. When John W. ordered Kevin and Wes to set prices for Mosaic's upcoming Fashion Show and then blindly trusted whatever numbers they chose, he was revealed in the boardroom as inexcusably out of touch. When Kelly and Sandy double-checked Maria's Bridal Shop e-mail blast and discovered that she'd left off a crucial phone number, they not only caught the mistake in time, they also showed the right way to delegate. Trust, but verify!

The women of Apex clearly don't consider Pamela a member of the team.

Pamela enjoys the loft's workout equipment one final time.

Stay Tuned

Some of the most promising applicants fell short when they failed to take the pulse of the people they were supposed to manage. A perfect example is Pamela. "I'm not rooting for uteruses versus penises," she said before taking charge of the all-female Apex. "I'm rooting for my team, whatever team that is, to win." Unfortunately for Pamela, the other women never saw her as part of the team at all. "Tonight in the boardroom it is really a decision between taking out Pamela or taking out one of us," said Ivana after Apex's loss, and no wonder: Pamela interacted with her teammates only long enough to boss them around. Typically, she held herself apart right until the end, obliviously pumping iron while the group formed a united front against her. "I don't think I'm cocky when I say that I'd be surprised if I got fired," Pamela boasted shortly before Trump lowered the boom. More time spent among the rank and file might have changed Pamela's perspective and given her a fighting chance to move on.

Raj proved Pamela's polar opposite during his second stint as project manager in the Home Improvement episode. Right at the start, he sat teammate Kevin down and asked point-blank, "How can I improve?" Raj wasn't afraid to hear what people thought of him, and he was wise enough to know that those opinions mattered. His connection with his fellow Apex members won him boardroom allies who fought for him to the finish, and the misjudgment that ultimately brought him low involved an underperforming subcontractor, not one of the teammates whom he'd learned to read so well.

Keep the Pecking Order Clear

It's best to draw the lines of authority in bold strokes. Project managers who failed to do so often lost time untangling them. These were some of the stickier snarls:

Heidi's "co-pilot" grabs the wheel away from her at the Jessica Simpson concert.

- Kwame had more faith in his "partner in combat," Troy, than anyone else, so when the going got tough in season one's climactic Jessica Simpson concert, Troy was often looking over Heidi or Omarosa's shoulder. To Heidi in particular, it felt like he was doing a lot more than looking—sometimes he was calling the shots. At the pre-concert meet and greet for which Heidi was responsible, she was caught off guard when the number of attendees swelled and only Troy was told in advance. Heidi complained to Kwame and got his promise that Troy was merely a "co-pilot," but the damage had been done. Time had been lost, feelings bruised, and a power dynamic between teammates established; even after Kwame's intervention, Troy still took up an awful lot of space at the meet and greet.

- Tara did a good job of delegating responsibility to Craig in the Graffiti Billboard episode, leaving him to supervise the painters while she planned the images for their colossal Gran Turismo 4 mural. Unfortunately, Tara neglected to mention Craig's authority to anyone but Craig. "I'm not one of his children," Audrey griped when Craig suddenly turned bossy. Craig lashed right back: "I don't need to deal with no children. I will sit their butt down." Tara made peace by backing Craig, but she could have spared Net Worth aggravation by making roles clear before conflict sparked.

Craig shows he's no pushover when Audrey balks at his instructions.

Demand Loyalty

- Bill vowed not to forget it after Katrina and Ereka ganged up on him in the Apartment Renovation episode's boardroom. "Screw me once, shame on you," he said. "Screw me twice, shame on me." When Ereka brought Bill back to the firing line after the following week's Trump Ice task, Bill paid her back with interest. Asked by Trump who should be fired, Bill chose Ereka rather than Nick. "You sold me out, Bill," Ereka complained as she headed for the elevator. "No I didn't," he replied. "Short-term memory."

- Perhaps nothing is more essential to a manager's success than spotting an Omarosa in the ranks. For nine episodes Omarosa seemed to pursue her own agenda rather than the group's. Whether playing basketball in the street moments after claiming to be too debilitated by concussion to pitch in on the Apartment Renovation or drawing kicks beneath the table from Amy by mishandling sales of Trump Ice, Omarosa appeared more interested in making the most of her moment in the reality TV spotlight than in getting the job done right. By the time Kwame chose her for his climactic Jessica Simpson Concert team, he'd had many chances to read the signs. But instead of double- and triple-checking her every move, Kwame stuck with his hands-off style and stayed out of the loop while she misplaced Jessica Simpson. Asked about a phone call from the Taj Mahal's event coordinator that was supposed to prevent that very thing, Omarosa pretended she'd never got it. Kwame realized that she was lying but kept her on the job. He lived to regret his choice when Mr. Trump asked to meet Jessica but Kwame couldn't find her. Meanwhile, Omarosa was with Jessica in the star's suite, trying on clothes instead of minding her walkie-talkie and her beeper. "This was the first time I thought I could be fired," Kwame said, and this time his instinct was right on the money. "Omarosa lied to you," Trump said as he chose Bill over Kwame as the ultimate winner. "Why didn't you fire her? When somebody deceives you, you have to do something." Kwame didn't demand loyalty, and because of that he would never be the Apprentice.

A Star Is Boring: Omarosa acts like center stage is wherever she happens to be.

> *"If somebody sabotages what you're doing, you don't handle it like a gentleman. You say, 'Get out of my face, I can't use you.'"*
>
> — George Ross

Focus on the Common Goal

Winners know when to set aside their differences. *Apprentice* applicants were both collaborators and competitors—and often had to switch back and forth between the two on a dime—so leaders who managed their emotions as effectively as their personnel were the ones left standing at the end.

Jennifer M. and Sandy pledged loyalty to one another mere minutes after this vicious boardroom battle.

- One of *The Apprentice*'s most heated shouting matches came in the Pepsi Edge episode's boardroom, where Sandy and Jennifer M. went at each other tooth and claw. When their slugfest unexpectedly KO'd Andy instead, the two women immediately shifted gears. By the time they got back to the suite, weeks of bitter words had been buried along with the proverbial hatchet. They went into the M-Azing Bar task trading kudos, and came out of it victorious after the M&M Sisters' perfectly coordinated sales pitch—and outfits and hairstyles—overcame Apex's superior numbers. Trump could hardly believe the change. "These were two people who hated each other two days ago, and now all of a sudden look at them," he marveled. "I've never seen anything like this." By concentrating on common interests rather than on petty grudges, Sandy and Jennifer had earned their places in the final four.

The will to win outweighs Troy's and Bill's differences in the Casino task.

- Bill was surprised when Troy and Kwame snatched him away from Versacorp to replenish the depleted Protégé. "Troy and I do not have compatible styles," Bill said. "Frankly, I'm not exactly fond of the way he does business." But any friction between the two was invisible once the Casino task began. In fact, Bill's strategic brilliance and Troy's irresistible hucksterism were perfectly matched as Versacorp targeted the most desirable gamblers and then bedazzled them with flash and fur (a giant roulette wheel and a white tiger). As Protégé roared to victory, project manager Kwame praised his colleagues' characters: "You just give them a mission . . . and they'll get it done." It was always easy to pick *The Apprentice*'s best out of any lineup.

"You hear it from me a lot: they've gotta be loyal. And you gotta be loyal to them too. People need security and they need to feel appreciated."

—George Steinbrenner

CHAPTER 8

ON LEADERSHIP

> *"The most important principle of leadership is knowing what you believe, because when you're in a crisis you have got to know what's really important to you."*
>
> —Rudy Giuliani

"Mr. Trump, I am a born leader." These words, spoken with typical confidence by Nick in season one, went to the heart of the *Apprentice* competition. Some candidates slipped beneath the radar, others toiled in the background, a few tried to complain their way to the top, but sooner or later the true leaders emerged from the pack. Here's what we learned from them.

R-E-S-P-E-C-T

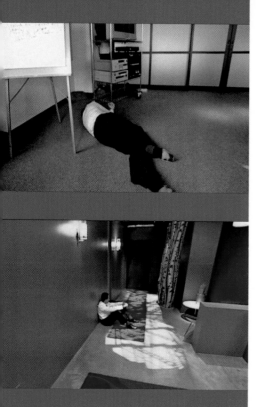

Two of Sam's finest moments

- Sam stole the show during season one's first three episodes with stunts like trying to sell a glass of lemonade for $1,000. He got himself noticed by Trump, who predicted that Sam's wild ideas would one day make him either a visionary leader or a guy who'd bring a company down in flames. But even as Sam raised his profile in the boardroom and on TV, he unwittingly destroyed any chance of his ultimate success. Antics like napping on the floor in the middle of a task and staging a sulky sit-in by the suite door because no one greeted him quickly convinced teammates that he was more of a mascot than a leader. At the eleventh hour, Sam finally wised up and complained, "I cannot lead until I have respect." But his awareness came too late: his teammates had handed him the project manager's job in the Buying Low episode in the hope that he'd fail and be fired. For once, Sam didn't let them down.

- Elizabeth took charge of a team full of powerful personalities for the NYPD Recruitment Campaign: Raj, Chris R., Maria, and Kevin each had the capacity to bulldoze a weak leader. She had to be strong or they'd eat her alive. Elizabeth held her ground during the initial brainstorming meeting, insisting on a non-military theme despite fierce resistance. But as time passed it became clear that she couldn't, or wouldn't, articulate a vision of her own. Sure enough, the alpha dogs began to bark. "I think we need to fire her," sniped Jennifer M. as the team's respect for its leader slipped away. Carolyn noted, "[Elizabeth's] inability to take a leadership role has led to animosity and disorganization in the team." Much more energy went into plotting Elizabeth's overthrow than into the task.

"The qualities that make a great leader? I'd say somebody who treats his associates with dignity and care so they're all on the same team. And he better be smart and not stubborn, and be ready to admit mistakes as soon as possible."

— "Ace" Greenberg
on Leadership

"The word leadership is always hard to define because you see so many people who are so different and they're great leaders. But the quality of a great leader that I've seen that's common to all is respect. People have to respect you or you cannot be a leader."

—Donald Trump

Can't Buy Me Love

Incentives can be powerful motivational tools, but they can also backfire. Bill drew cheers from the Planet Hollywood staff when he offered hourly $100 cash bonuses to the waiter who rang up the most sales; weeks later, Troy energized his Pedicab Fleet with a similar plan. But when an overcaffeinated Andy dangled dollars in front of corporate staffers during a late-night Pepsi Edge bottle-design marathon, he earned only scorn from designers and teammates alike. Cash incentives were inappropriate in that setting, and Andy's failure to respect the workplace culture made him look inexperienced and out of step. That impression only deepened when he withheld the staff's dinner until they'd met his goals. Small wonder the designers saddled him with a bottle that made marketing executives wince! Holding pizza hostage? What are they teaching at Harvard these days?

> *"You have to show you have confidence in [the team's] abilities. If you put them together you must have confidence in their abilities. Think big, act big, be big— Norman Vincent Peale used to say that."*
>
> —George Steinbrenner

Watch Your Mouth!

- Season one winner Bill Rancic carried himself with a leader's poise not only during the tasks but also during downtime. Even in the heat of his Pedicab Fleet quarrel with Katrina, Bill managed his mouth as effectively as he managed his teammate's resentment. It was easy to imagine him right at home on the other side of the boardroom table.

  It's unlikely that anyone would say the same about Heidi. Bill's fellow season one applicant had an affinity for colorful expletives, and teammates who rubbed her the wrong way were sure to hear a few. When Omarosa forced her to stop for lunch, Heidi turned bluer than Lenny Bruce. Heidi's salty tongue let others know that she was a tough customer, but it also raised questions about her suitability for the top job. Granted, Omarosa could probably draw a few unprintables from anybody. But Donald Trump wants executives who keep their cool; you don't hear Carolyn dropping the "f-bomb" every time the going gets tough. Mind your manners even off the clock.

Bill buttons his lip as Katrina boils over.

- In the Nescafé Taster's Choice episode, Danny's only confident executive decision was that Michael had to get off his butt. Secure in his exemption from being fired after the previous week's victory, Michael put in a lackluster effort that dragged down team morale. When Danny, the project manager and self-styled Magna "morale officer," confronted him head-on, Michael erupted in a profane tirade and threatened to throw Danny out a window. It was impossible to take Michael seriously after that; in fact, the whole team later banded together to tell him so. Michael vowed to reform, but the damage was done. He was an obvious lame duck, and the ax fell soon after.

It's Michael's image that goes out the window when he threatens Danny.

Ereka loses her cool . . .

. . . and her job.

"Keeping my composure I learned with experience and time. Whereas in my younger days (which weren't that long ago!), I perhaps did get a little emotional and I'd wake up the next morning and think to myself, 'Well, that wasn't very good for my career.' Now keeping my composure is very easy."

—Carolyn Kepcher

Control Your Emotions

Donald Trump has often said that passion is essential for success. But if you're not careful, runaway emotion can be hazardous to your professional health. Ereka came unglued in the Trump Ice episode, and the task slipped away along with her self-control. The first sign of trouble came during the planning phase, when she let her personal conflict with Bill prejudice her against his good ideas; she shut him down instead of capitalizing on his experience in building new businesses. Next she became visibly upset, almost tearful, right in front of Carolyn when the team's paperwork was in shambles at the task's final deadline. Finally, and fatally, she protected her friend Katrina by sending her to the suite when everyone—including Trump—knew she belonged in the boardroom. Ereka's loss of composure lost her the opportunity to become the Apprentice.

"Sometimes I don't keep cool and then I spank myself because I know I'm wrong. If I can't show coolness under pressure, then [the team] can't be expected to. People have to feel safe, that you know what you're doing, that you understand that they'll do their best.

—George Steinbrenner

Celebrate
Your Colleagues' Strengths

When Amy had the idea to sell advertising space on her team's Pedicab Fleet, project manager Bill positively beamed. He put all his energy behind the idea and gave her full credit for it. After their victory, Bill looked more than ever like a front-runner: his air of authority in the face of a strong collaborator—and competitor—showed a leader's confidence. In season one's final showdown with Kwame, Bill couldn't wait to get Amy on his team. "Amy's always made me elevate my game," he explained. "I've risen to the challenge."

Even as Bill cemented his leadership credentials, Katrina did the opposite. She bristled when Bill chose Amy's Pedicab idea over her own and had a testy give-and-take with him afterward. She was still stewing days later—even though the idea proved successful and Katrina shared in the victory. "Amy needs to be the star of every transaction," Katrina snipped, as she waited hopefully for Amy's comeuppance. Katrina's envy made her look small. By refusing to celebrate her colleague's strength, she revealed her own weakness.

Whether as colleagues or competitors, Bill and Amy push one another to greater heights.

Be Accountable

- Project manager Troy was, in his words, "looking up the ass of a dead dog with fleas" after Bill's Pedicab Fleet handed him one of season one's worst drubbings. But back in the boardroom, Troy chose not to point fingers. Instead, he calmly explained his strategy and accepted full responsibility for it. He recognized that Mosaic's sale of advertising space on their pedicabs was a brilliant move and that he'd been outfoxed. By the meeting's end, Troy's "the buck stops here" attitude had burnished his reputation as a leader even in defeat. Heidi, who had done no grievous wrong but who had never once stepped up and made herself accountable, was the recipient of The Donald's dreaded pronouncement.

"I tell the people here never give a client an excuse, you're just adding fuel to the flame. Say 'I was dumb, I made a mistake and I'll try to make it up to you.' That's all. When you make excuses for something you've done with a client, you're just going to inflame him. It's just going to get worse."

— "Ace" Greenberg
on Excuses

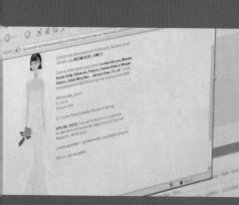

Maria proved that the coverup's worse than the crime when she lied about botching Mosaic's blast.

You Can't Fire Me, I Just Fired Myself! Brian beats Mr. Trump to the punch with an unprecedented self-sacking.

"There's an old saying: Ducks quack and eagles soar. Try to make yourself an eagle."

—George Steinbrenner

- In season two's finale, Jennifer M. alienated Trump—and the majority of the live audience—by not owning up to her error in neglecting the Genworth executives during her management of their Charity Basketball Classic. "I don't see how that's possible," she insisted despite George's first-hand account of the sponsor's complaints. In that same meeting, Kelly took heat for headquartering himself away from the action during the Polo Cup's first hour. Unlike Jennifer, Kelly stepped up to the plate, acknowledged his missteps, and won.

- Maria swore that she had included a phone number on Mosaic's Bridal Shop e-mail blast, but somehow the announcement had gone out without one. It was a colossal speed bump for a team that had been cruising toward a win. An investigation revealed that Maria had, in fact, signed off on the flawed e-mail, then lied about it to escape blame. Her bid to escape accountability succeeded only in making her look less like a leader. "I just hate it when people don't take accountability," snarled Sandy.

- Anyone could have been fired when Trump summoned both Magna and Net Worth to the boardroom after each produced horrendous commercials for the launch of Dove Cool Moisture body wash. Trump quickly zeroed in on the quarrelsome Net Worth rather than on the harmonious Magna, and project manager Kristen found herself under fire. Even as more and more teammates revealed that she had ruled with an iron grip, Kristen insisted that she bore no responsibility for the loss. She attacked teammate Audrey rather than take accountability. A good offense isn't always the best defense, however: Kristen was soon venting her indignation in the backseat of the taxi that carried her off the show.

The Schmuck Stops Here

Accountability is important, but don't get carried away. Brian shot himself in the foot when in the Motel Hell episode's boardroom he actually told Trump to fire him. That's not accountability, that's self-destruction.

"I've seen people go forty-eight hours and even more, days and days without any sleep in order to get a deal done. Sometimes you have to do that. And if you don't have the physical or mental stamina to do it, guess what, you better be doing something else."

—Donald Trump

Walk the Talk

- For his final showdown with Kwame at the end of season one, Bill led three recently fired applicants into the whirlwind of the Chrysler Trump Golf Tournament and emerged victorious. How did he draw a winning effort from people with nothing to gain, two of whom had just been eliminated earlier that very episode? By getting up at 4:30 A.M., giving the task 1,000 percent, and even picking through the trash to find a sponsor's missing sign. Bill led by example, and his teammates took pride in keeping up. "Nick, Amy, and I are no longer competing," said Katrina. "We're all trying to achieve the same goal for one person.

- Jennifer C.'s example in the Restaurant Opening episode provoked a very different response. Her lack of organization and ferocious personal battles with teammate Stacy R. further dispirited an Apex squad already demoralized by three consecutive losses. "I don't think Jen C. inspired us," said Jennifer M. "I think we launched the restaurant in spite of Jen C." For once, Ivana and Jennifer M. were in perfect agreement. "I think if we pull it off, it's not going to be because of her leadership skills," Ivana said. After Apex's unsurprising loss, Bill gave a blunt boardroom critique: "Jen needed to lead more by example rather than just standing in a corner and delegating. She didn't do anything." Jen C.'s example led her team in precisely the wrong direction.

- Kendra got it half right in the Pontiac Solstice Brochure episode when she single-handedly brought home the win for Magna with a brilliant all-night design marathon. As the hour grew late and the teams hunkered down to work until dawn, Net Worth's Bren thought victory was in the bag. "Tana and Craig are not familiar with the concept of an all-nighter," he sneered as, sure enough, Magna's more mature members faded with the sunlight. Under the guise of deferring to their project manager's greater experience in the field, Tana and Craig went home to sleep with the job nowhere near finished. Kendra was aghast. "The project manager is

Bill gets his hands dirty during the hunt for Marquis Jet's sign.

Tana gets her beauty rest while project manager Kendra pulls an all-nighter.

not the one who does everything while you do nothing and go home and get your beauty rest," she correctly declared. Unfortunately, she was speaking to the cameraman when she should have been speaking to her teammates. Instead, she let them leave her in the lurch to then return the next morning refreshed and ready to soak up an undeserved share of the credit. Who had managed whom? If past seasons' winners could motivate staffers with scores to settle and nothing to gain, surely a good leader would have found a way to keep her crew out from under the blankets. When Tana and Craig's best efforts could not be inspired, it should have been demanded. Kendra was rightly hailed for her Solstice Brochure effort; never before on *The Apprentice* had an applicant shouldered such a disproportionate share of the workload. But the traits that she exhibited were those of a great worker, not a great leader. Kendra declared this episode her "time to shine," and she shone very brightly indeed, but in the middle of the night when no one could see. Leadership by example fails if no one follows. She should have been a little more "show-me" and a little less "I'll-show-them." Kendra walked the walk superbly, but she shouldn't have walked alone.

An Ounce of Prevention Is Worth a Pound of Cure

Kwame was a coolheaded master of damage control. He didn't even break a sweat during season one's finale when his team misplaced Jessica Simpson—not once but twice: first en route from the airport and next in the Taj Mahal when Mr. Trump's star attraction was nowhere to be found when he wanted to say hello. No matter what the problem, Kwame swooped in with a solution. Too many fans at Jessica Simpson's meet and greet? No problem: Kwame ordered them ushered through in smaller groups. No food at the headliner's breakfast? He was right there to soothe ruffled feathers. So if keeping a level head under pressure is a hallmark of good leadership, why did Kwame look so bad? Because every one of his problems was avoidable. He left Omarosa in charge of keeping tabs on Jessica even after she'd botched the job once, and continued to give work to Troy even after things started falling through the cracks. Proactive problem solving would have made for a smoother event, and maybe won Kwame a job as the Apprentice.

Kwame puts out fires as fast as Omarosa can set them at the Jessica Simpson concert, but his mellow management leaves the team uninspired.

Send a Clear Message

Bill was a man on the go at the Chrysler Trump Golf Tournament. He was everywhere at once, overseeing teammates, shaking sponsors' hands, rocketing in and out of the clubhouse at a near-sprint. "I'm always doing a hundred things at once," he explained. "I like to operate at a fast pace." But, unknown to Bill, his team perceived him as "frenzied" and "panicked" and predicted that he'd lose the task.

Meanwhile, at the Jessica Simpson concert Kwame refused to micromanage. If Troy, Heidi, or Omarosa said something was going to be done, he trusted their word. "My leadership style requires talented people," he said. "I put faith in the fact that I think that they're competent." Later on in the boardroom, however, his team said he lacked passion and needed to be more hands-on. Neither Bill nor Kwame saw himself through his teammates' eyes until after the wrong message had been sent.

Bill burns enough energy to thaw Trump National's frozen turf, but teammates wonder if he's finally lost his cool.

> *"When something's going wrong, if the leader doesn't get up and straighten it out or doesn't indicate that it's going wrong, then you're not really leading."*
>
> —George Ross

> *"The leader that wants to be popular—that wants to be loved—that leader ultimately is not going to make it."*
>
> —Donald Trump

Don't Go Changing to Try and Please Me

Jennifer M. didn't win any popularity contests: "She thrives on confrontation," groaned Chris R.; "I don't care for Jen very much," growled Trump COO Matthew Calamari; "She's abrasive as hell," agreed George. Yet week after week she held on as the applicants' ranks thinned. Asked by Trump in the Pepsi Edge episode's boardroom how she kept sliding by, Jennifer answered that she did good work and her teammates knew it. Project manager Andy, even with his own job on the line, couldn't help but agree. During season two's finale, the live audience snickered when the kindest thing said about Jennifer M. was that she motivated people who didn't like her. But as one of only two applicants still at the table, Jennifer had the last laugh.

Beware Overconfidence

- Sandy was all smiles when Trump announced the Bridal Shop episode's task. "You've got to be kidding," she said, as her teammates celebrated. A bridal salon owner by trade, Sandy was Mosaic's "ringer." Even Trump spoke as if the win was in the bag. "If you lose this time, this would not be good," he ribbed. But Sandy didn't let overconfidence undo her; instead, she set out to bury the competition—and did. She threw herself into the procurement of dresses, told Wes and Maria how to send an e-mail blast, saved the day after they botched the blast anyway, and still found the energy to ream out project manager Kelly for not cracking the whip ("There's no hustling!" she fumed). Sandy's teammates may have been overconfident, but their ringer was anything but. Mosaic rode her expertise—and killer instinct—to a lopsided victory.

- Overconfidence was a killer in the Trump Ice episode when Nick brushed off Ereka's order to educate himself about the next day's customers. The cocky copier salesman thought he knew everything there was to know about closing deals, but New York's merchants proved him dead wrong. When Versacorp finished behind Protégé, Nick had plenty to answer for. Although Nick's self-possession ultimately saved him in the boardroom, a dose of humility might have kept him from being there in the first place.

Set a Positive Tone

Chris R. stuck his neck out at the end of the Home Improvement episode when he warned Mr. Trump that Apex's awful chemistry would continue to drag the team down. In response, The Donald ordered Chris to take charge of the next task and warned, "I will be watching you very closely." The following week, it was do or die for Chris. As Bridal Shop project manager, he started off with a down-beat motivational speech and things only deteriorated from there.

Chris R.'s fighting spirit deserts him like a runaway bride just hours into the Bridal Shop task.

"How can Chris really be an effective project manager when he obviously feels so negative about the team?" Jennifer M. wondered. After salon owners spurned Chris's uncharacteristically lackluster phone pitches, he pronounced the task "impossible" and forecast a net loss for both squads. His teammates were appalled. "To throw up your hands that early in the game is pathetic," said Ivana. Before heading out to meet vendors face-to-face, Apex literally had to talk its project manager off the floor. Small wonder Trump soon put Chris out of his misery. "Impossible" doesn't belong in any project manager's vocabulary.

"It does, in fact, start from the top and I filter down a very positive energy. We all work as a team at Trump National Golf Courses and nobody ever says 'That's not part of my job description.' And the second part of that—and I make this abundantly clear—if you don't want to be here, I don't want you here. I want you to enjoy what you do because if you enjoy what you do you're going to take pride in it, and if you take pride in it, you're going to be very successful."

—Carolyn on Positivity

Stand Your Ground

Andy knew that his vision for the NYPD Recruitment Campaign was a winner, but his older, more experienced teammates had their doubts. The objections began even as Andy unveiled the big emotional questions that would be the project's backbone. Kelly rolled his eyes. Maria blinked hers. The team complained in front of George that the concept had no sex appeal. Maria thought it would be hot to feature a Hummer, proving that she's never had to park next to one in Manhattan. But Andy didn't yield an inch. By the task's finish, Mosaic's naysayers were reduced to ineffectual grousing among themselves, while Andy edited the ad that Donnie Deutsch pronounced the winner by a landslide.

On the same task, rival project manager Elizabeth knew what she didn't want. "Scare tactics don't work," she declared, nixing her team's demand for a military theme. "I'm not going to change my mind." But under fire from Apex's domineering personalities ("It's not a friggin' tampon commercial!" snarled Chris), that's exactly what she did. "I will go with the group," she conceded during the brainstorming session. "If you guys feel that strongly about it." When she later supported Kevin's last-minute non-military idea, Elizabeth had one more opportunity to take a stand. But when the team gave the new approach a hostile reception, Elizabeth backed down again. She'd lost her last chance to remain true to herself—and survive until the next task.

Prioritize

As Kevin said, "A leader stays where he's needed," and the best project managers always seemed to know exactly where that was. The others? Well . . .

- Time was running short before Mosaic's Fashion Show, so when designer Ilsa made her last stitch, project manager John W. grabbed an armload of clothes and bolted for the runway. Almost as an afterthought, he gave Kevin and Wes responsibility for setting the line's price. They overpriced big-time, and in the boardroom it was John who took the fall. "You had absolutely no involvement in the pricing, and as the project manager that's just inexcusable," Trump admonished.

> *"Never get sidetracked by less important tasks. Always focus on the goal. If you do get sidetracked, get right back on the rails, because ultimately sidetracking kills you."*
>
> —Donald Trump

Tana and Alex go "hella far" for a BeDazzler.

Kendra takes a break from quarreling with Craig to mobilize Romero Britto's fan base.

All That Glitters Isn't Sold

The evening Alex and Tana spent fetching rhinestones from Staten Island rather than planning marketing strategy proved their undoing in the Hanes T-Shirt episode. Net Worth's spangled stars looked great on their pricey limited-edition product, but customers were scarce. Rivals Kendra and Craig bickered like an old married couple but balanced their time between working with their artist, Romero Britto, and figuring out how to attract his fans. An e-mail to art lovers brought in enough traffic to offset the team's lower prices, and Magna scored the win. "We missed the market," conceded Alex in what would be his series swan song. "We sold T-shirts but we didn't sell art." Carolyn spelled out Net Worth's error: "You spent so much time designing the shirt but you didn't utilize the artist, you didn't utilize anything to do with marketing." By traveling too far for a fistful of baubles, Alex and Tana allowed the task to slip through their fingers.

- During the Basketball Classic, Jennifer M. missed the forest for the trees. She stayed up late to print signs for her clients but missed the signs that her clients sent her, such as Genworth's executives' lack of faith in her leadership. She got NBA commissioner David Stern to emcee the event, then handed the microphone over to Pamela to introduce him. In fact, Pamela's was by far the most visible presence at the game, a fact that Trump noted while making his final choice between Jennifer and Kelly. He also expressed his displeasure at Jennifer's neglect after the game, when he "stood there like an idiot" expecting someone—anyone—to check in. Jen insisted that she'd been behind the scenes putting out fires, but she wound up scorched by her failure to be in the right places—such as at Mr. Trump's side.

Jennifer M. stays behind the scenes at the Basketball Classic—and others get the applause.

- "I have notes I'm doing here," Todd scolded when Alex interrupted him early on in the Burger King episode. Todd pored over paperwork and fretted about Danny's nonexistent marketing strategy instead of supervising Alex, whom he'd put in charge of production and sales. Staying out of the loop in these crucial departments cost Todd dearly when there were too few cashiers to handle the lunchtime rush. Untrained in register operation—or any other production job—himself, Todd could only watch as frustrated customers took their business elsewhere.

Turn Around, Todd: Magna's project manager works the phone instead of learning how to work the register.

Watch Your Values

Pamela was a force to reckon with early on in season two, but she stumbled badly in the QVC TV episode after Trump made her switch teams and take charge of the free-falling Apex. Among other missteps, she revealed an alarmingly casual attitude toward the rules. After telling Stacy R. to get the QVC attorney's approval for their live televised sales pitch, she criticized her for being too careful. "We are not here to be legally thorough," Pamela sneered. "We want to get him to 'Yes,' however we do it." Stacy stifled her objections but later let Pamela have it in the boardroom. "I'm not going to act unethically," she announced. "If you want another Enron on your hands, Mr. Trump, here's Pamela." It was the beginning of the end for the previously untarnished Pamela. Never downsize your scruples.

"The only advice I can really give you: don't ever compromise on your standards or your objectives, because the worst thing is to compromise and lose."

—Michael Bloomberg, Mayor, New York City

"Oftentimes you'll have an idea and you'll fall in love with it. And then it turns out to be not such a good idea, and you can't get rid of it. When the idea turns out bad, cut it out of your mind. Go on to the next thing and let it be better."

—Donald Trump

Recognize When You've Made a Bad Choice

Bradford, Apex's only male, came across like a chauvinist during his reign as project manager on the Child's Play episode. Tasked with the invention of a new Mattel product for boys, he brushed aside his teammates' unanimous favorite—a remote-controlled car with interchangeable parts—in favor of his own idea: a maneuverable plastic football player's head. The women were outraged—Maria wished her hands were around his throat—but Bradford's "executive decision" steamrolled them all. When Mattel's designers gave his idea the thumbs-down, however, Bradford immediately changed gears. Without hesitation or apparent shame, he smoothly dropped his original pitch and instead presented the women's concept. The "Metamorphor" was a hit with designers and children alike. Bradford's willingness to suspend his ego helped Apex notch season two's first win.

Give Credit Where Credit Is Due

"I don't know why I don't get how this works," complained Jennifer M. when Ivana introduced the "fit wheel" to Apex. Jennifer's teammates shared laughs at her expense after every attempt to make her understand fell short. But there was no laughter later on when Jennifer stole Ivana's credit for the fit wheel concept during the team's presentation to Levi's president Robert Hanson. Hanson was impressed and sang her praises to Trump, but Jennifer's treachery had a price: she went into the next task with teammates who were unshakably united against her.

In contrast, when Mosaic won the QVC TV tasks, thanks to Kelly's insistence on a high price for their panini grill, project manager Chris R. didn't hide his delight. Quick to give creit where it was due, he high-fived Kelly right in front of The Donald, a gesture that saluted achievement and also sent a message about Chris's style of leadership. Both men looked like winners.

Leadership from Below

It's said that nature abhors a vacuum, and so does a team, especially when that vacuum is at the top. When a leader falters, there are a number of ways to go. You can do nothing, like Kelly in the M-Azing Bar episode when it became clear that Ivana's street savvy didn't equal Jennifer M.'s and Sandy's. Kelly had been a take-charge kind of guy all season long, but this time he seemed unusually content to lie back and watch the competition sell circles around him. After all, it wasn't his neck that was on the line. He had an exemption and would be going to the final four no matter what. George noted his passivity and brought it up in the boardroom. Kelly skated by, but on uncharacteristically thin ice.

> *"Say it like it is. Direct. But think carefully about what you're going to say and then back it up. If you say 'I'm not getting what I want' and the boss says 'What aren't you getting?' you better have the answer and you better have examples. Don't just go in and wing it and make general statements. You gotta be specific."*
>
> —George Ross
> on Talking to the Boss

> *"You have to find a way to communicate with your CEO or leader and convince him or her that a change is necessary. To stay on a path of destruction doesn't work."*
>
> —Allen Weisselberg, Chief Financial Officer, The Trump Organization

John G. looks like a bozo when he tries to bully his way out of wearing a clown suit.

Insurrection's another option. *The Apprentice* saw a few open rebellions when uncertain leaders lost their grip on the wheel. Kevin told Elizabeth to "Shut up!" when she gave one vague instruction too many in the NYPD Recruitment episode. Worse, John G. told Net Worth project manager Audrey, "You're an idiot!" when she ordered him into a clown suit to hand out flyers for the team's miniature golf course. In both cases the team leaders were indeed falling down on the job. But by blowing their stacks both men looked like part of the problem rather than its solution. And John had to wear that clown suit anyway, including the big red nose. There are productive alternatives to pretending that you don't see anything or waging open warfare.

Kelly raised eyebrows—and his profile—by taking over design duties when others faltered.

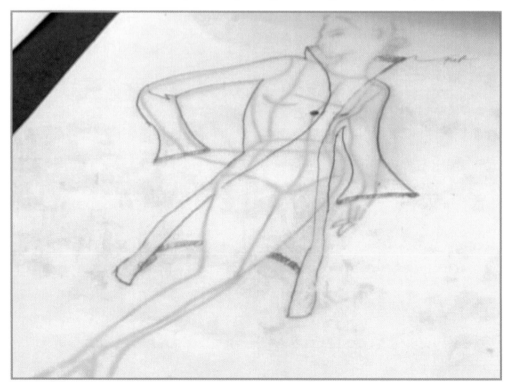

Show

Kelly led by example even when he didn't have to in the Fashion Show episode. Frustrated by project manager John W.'s inability to get the team's clothing designs done, Kelly grabbed a pencil and sketched out a cape himself. Chris joked that the former military man might wear "pink camouflage underwear," but Kevin and others recognized that the true leader in their ranks was not the man with the title.

Tell

Alex modeled an even better path in the Nescafé Taster's Choice episode when Danny's refusal to make choices pushed Magna to the brink of disaster. An event planner had named a high price for satisfying the team's need for a coffee buzz, and Danny didn't want to make the call by himself. While he agonized, precious time slipped away. The team still had no promotional concept and couldn't afford the delay. Finally, Alex took action. He drew Danny aside and told him exactly what the team needed. "Make a decision," Alex advised. "There's no choice." Alex was direct but completely professional. His tone was unemotional. He stayed focused on the behavior and didn't make it personal. Danny got the message and took action. Alex had led his leader out of the doldrums.

"Perseverance is very important. You set the goal, put your mind to it, just don't pay [attention to] what anybody tells you. Donald is a great example of it. I knew Donald when he was at the top, when he was at the bottom, and now he's climbed back up to the top again. You can never give up on yourself."

—George Steinbrenner

CHAPTER 9

SHOWMANCE, ROMANCE, AND OTHER OFFICE RELATIONSHIPS

Season one had more leg than an ostrich farm, deployed, for the most part, to help bilk the unwary out of their hard-earned cash. Such is one's God-given right as an American capitalist. But fans who hypothetically, say, slo-moed every suite scene in the hope of catching Jessie in her sleepwear couldn't help but wonder what went on behind the scenes. Even if there were no sordid blooper reel trysts, viewers saw enough to learn that the careful management of workplace relationships—romantic or otherwise—can make or break a rising star.

Separate Business from Personal

To do well on *The Apprentice*, one had to take the show's motto, "It's not personal, it's just business," to heart. Applicants who checked their feuds and friendships at the boardroom door were most likely to keep their heads off Trump's chopping block.

- In the Penthouse Rental episode, three of *The Apprentice*'s toughest competitors—Troy, Kwame, and Bill—met an unexpected defeat when Amy and Nick found a deep-pocketed bidder at the last minute. Forced to choose between his good friend Kwame and a man with whom he'd had a prickly relationship—Bill—project manager Troy took the former into the boardroom with him. The Donald was surprised. Not only had Troy chosen his friend, but Kwame didn't seem to mind. The pair had healthy boundaries when it came to their personal and professional affairs. As Troy put it, "Business is business. Friends are friends. Don't use them in the same sentence." Although Kwame ultimately bested his buddy in boardroom combat, Troy gave himself a fighting chance by setting friendship aside and choosing the more vulnerable opponent.

"I used to do a lot of business with Donald when he first got started, and then everybody wanted to do business with him and they were giving him propositions that were ridiculous— good for him but bad for the people making the offers. And I said, 'Donald, go ahead, do it with them. It's not going to hurt my feelings. They're offering you dumb deals on their part, so take advantage of them.' Which he did, of course. It didn't affect our friendship."

— "Ace" Greenberg on Doing Business With Friends

- What sealed Jennifer C.'s doom in the Restaurant Opening episode was not only her notorious rant against old Jewish ladies but her inability to keep the personal bitterness that followed from affecting her business decisions. Jennifer caused controversy (and got herself fired from her real-life job) when she vented her frustration at a pair of diners whom she assumed had badmouthed her to the Zagat guide. "It was those two old Jewish bat ladies," she fumed to her Apex colleagues. "They were like the pinnacle of the New York jaded old bags. Old JAPs who talk that [bleep] about the decor can kiss my ass." When Stacy R. took issue with her project manager's tirade, *she* became its target. Jennifer insisted that their conflict wasn't personal, but her middle-school-maturity-level taunts—"You know what's funny is that you think you're popular and liked!"—told a different story. So great was Jennifer's fury that she couldn't wait to drag Stacy before Trump, despite crystal-clear warnings from the other side of the boardroom table that it was a mistake. "Sounds personal," remarked Carolyn when Stacy was put on the firing line. When Jennifer still didn't get it, Bill Rancic (this time from Trump's side of the boardroom table) spelled it out. "This is not a game," he cautioned. "Pulling people into the boardroom for the wrong reason—that's the quickest way to go home." But Jennifer would not be deterred. Not surprisingly, when The Donald gave her the boot he zeroed in on her selection of boardroom companions as his main reason: "You had a chance to bring in one person who really did mess up—it was Sandy—and you chose not to do that." Jennifer should have shelved her beefs with Jewish women, especially the one who undid her in the boardroom.

Ivana refuses to return fire when Stacie J. tries to launch "word war two."

- One disgraced applicant found redemption, while another reopened old wounds when Trump brought back four fired cast members in season two's Home Improvement episode. Rob, who hadn't made much of an impression before being sacked in the season opener, came back determined to set things right. Rather than try to settle scores with those who'd made him the fall guy, he threw himself into the house-renovation project with gusto even though it seemed he had little to gain. The payoff came in the boardroom. Trump, who'd previously questioned Rob's work ethic, now saw him differently. "I like Rob," he declared. "What spirit, huh?" By focusing on business, Rob proved himself to be a valuable asset.

    The Donald had kind words for Stacie J. as well, but behind the scenes it was the same old same old. "This is your time to redeem yourself," Chris R. had told her early on, and at first Stacie seemed to agree. "I have to rebuild and recoup my name in front of all these business associates," she said as she returned to the suite for the first time since her bitter second-episode exit. Once there, however, Stacie reverted to form. Under the guise of setting the record straight, she was soon showering Ivana with abuse. "You're chaotic, indecisive, disorganized, and look—you walk away from me every time!" she shouted, as Ivana demonstrated precisely why she was still in the hunt and Stacie was not. Given a chance to show that she'd learned to separate business from personal, Stacie instead showed the opposite.

Office Romance

Amy and Nick unwittingly illustrated the profits and perils of workplace flirtation with their season one escapades. When it was all over, Amy dismissed her apparent on-air dalliance with Nick as a "showmance," a carefully edited producer's concoction brewed to spice up the series. Nevertheless, viewers liked to imagine there was more to the story. Clearly there was an attraction. "She's a great girl," gushed Nick. "Very, very pretty, and she's intelligent as well. She reminds me of my mom."

At the very least, two strong competitors blurred the line between business and personal for mutual gain. "I focus [on] aligning myself with the strongest team members until the end, and then from that point I think it's my responsibility to work on my own," said Amy, explaining her strategy. For his part, Nick got to hitch his wagon to a woman whose ten-task winning streak remains unmatched by any *Apprentice* candidate. "Amy's a very strong player and it's good to be semi-aligned with her," he said. And indeed the two helped each other excel. Amy never looked better than when Nick picked her to join his team in the Art Gallery episode. "Don't you think you're giving Amy too much power?" Trump asked him. "Maybe what you're telling me is I should just give her the job right now."

But when the relationship came to light, Amy paid a price. Fighting for her life in the boardroom after the Casino task, Katrina accused Amy of protecting Nick for personal reasons. Trump seemed taken aback. "I'm surprised at you Amy," he said, "I didn't see this." After that Amy heard very little about her business successes and a whole lot about Nick. "You think you and Amy might someday live in a place like that together as man and wife?" joked Trump after the couple toured the Trump World Tower's penthouse. When they boarded his private jet for a flight to Mar-a-Lago, he ribbed, "They better not use my bedroom." Even a rumored office romance was enough to knock Amy off the fast track and back into the pack. Think carefully before taking a workplace relationship that extra step.

"That's human nature. We like romance."

—George Ross

Know the Social Alignments

Ivana thought Jennifer M.'s "hypnotic fembot spell" was the reason Chris R. spared her the boardroom after the Bridal Shop episode. The truth is, Chris had bigger problems. He just didn't know it yet. If he'd looked at recent history, he might have spared himself some grief, and Jennifer might not have had such a relaxing evening. Ivana and Kevin shared a friendship and mutual respect and had just looked out for each other in the previous episode's boardroom. Raj wasn't the easiest person to outmaneuver but the pair managed it, and he of the immaculately knotted bow tie was the one who took the fall. Chris never should have marched to Trump's table with these two closely aligned competitors in tow. If he'd brought in Jennifer, everyone would have ganged up on her. Instead, Chris was the one to face a united front. "Frankly, I might have fired Jennifer if you didn't let her go," said Trump before he sent Chris to the street. Chris had acted as if friendships never matter, and sometimes they do.

Recognize Friendship's Perils

Even a non-romantic workplace relationship can take its toll. Several *Apprentice* hopefuls learned that the hard way.

- Good friends Kwame and Troy had watched each other's back all season long, so it must have been hard for Kwame to crack down when his buddy got in over his head at the Jessica Simpson concert. Because Omarosa was such a disaster, it was easy to overlook how many things Troy did wrong. He didn't make sure the Taj Mahal's kitchen knew when to bring Jessica's breakfast, he angered Heidi by taking over the meet and greet she was supposed to direct, and he let Omarosa slip away with the singer when Kwame and Trump were looking for her. It was only natural that when crunch time came Kwame turned to the person he trusted most. But Kwame kept acting like a friend when what Troy needed was a boss.

- Likewise, Ivana lost control of her friend Kevin in the M-Azing Bar episode and didn't know how to get him back. First Kevin slowed down the assembly line in the M&M/Mars factory without getting Ivana's okay. Ivana complained, but to the camera rather than to her pal. After the team took to the street—with disappointingly few bars—Kevin again took matters into his own hands when sales were slow by dropping his price to $1. And again Ivana failed to assert herself. Ultimately, Ivana discovered that it was easier to whip off her skirt than to demand cooperation from a friend.

Kevin does things his way—with or without Ivana's permission.

Audrey rejects John's attempt at reconciliation.

Address Personal Conflicts Before They Spill Over

Viewers loved it when *The Apprentice* focused on the suite spats. Watching John G. trade insults with Audrey was a lot more entertaining than watching Bren teach Alex how to smoke a cigar. What wasn't so easy to watch was the fallout after personal conflicts raged out of control. Ultimately, the "havoc-wreakers" (to quote Jennifer C.) fell into one of two categories: those who made peace and those who got burned.

Productive Play— Three Views on Golf

"Golf is an amazing game. I've seen people become tremendous friends on a golf course, whereas when they go out for lunch or dinner they can't stand each other."
—Donald Trump

"How often can you get a client out for a good three hours, have no phones ringing, nobody bothering you, just walking out in the clean fresh air getting some exercise and have that person's attention for that long period of time in a very social, casual, comfortable setting? You don't have that too often, especially in New York City offices."
—Carolyn Kepcher

"I think if I did that with the people I've been involved with they'd kill each other with the golf clubs. I wouldn't try that at all, not with these gorillas."
—"Ace" Greenberg

- Audrey passed up a chance to mend fences with John in the Miniature Golf episode and later paid the price. Audrey took a lot of flak from teammates in season three's early episodes, but John's condescension seemed to hurt the most. After escaping a bruising boardroom in the Graffiti Billboard episode, she vented to Angie and Chris, telling them about the toughness she'd acquired as a child with both parents in prison and a face so beautiful it made other kids hate her. "I have tried and tried and tried my entire life for people just to accept me!" Audrey pleaded. But there was no accepting John's olive branch when he joined the conversation. "We're all on the same team," John said. "My fate is involved in the happiness of this team as much as anybody else's." But Audrey stormed away with an emphatic "[Bleep] you!" The two then turned the Miniature Golf episode into their private little war, and the team's confidence in Audrey's leadership, never high, eroded further. "You were content to fail because you wanted to bring me to the boardroom to get me fired," accused John in front of Trump. His words rang true. Though it might have been a bitter pill to swallow, taking John's hand when he extended it would have served Audrey well.

"Get it away from the business environment. Take 'em out to dinner, take 'em out to lunch. Take in the ball game. Find out what their likes and dislikes are and try to do that. Maybe they like to go fishing. Whatever it is that would get them out of the business environment and into a feeling of relaxation. If they're relaxed and they see another side of you then the tendency is that they will not be as difficult to work with."

—George Ross on Calming the Waters

• In contrast, Stephanie took the bull by the horns when her teammates told her they were sick of her negativity in the Business on Wheels boardroom. Afterward, Stephanie surprised them by telling them they were right. "I appreciate the constructive criticism," she told her shocked colleagues. "I'm here to learn, and grow, from the most successful people in the United States." Stephanie's disarming humility (not to mention flattery) erased any lingering resentment and changed Magna's view of her for the better. "Oh my gosh, did you guys think I was gonna be like a total bitch or something?" asked Stephanie—to a chorus of yeses. By making peace instead of trouble, Stephanie had turned her *Apprentice* experience around.

The queen havoc-wreaker was, of course, Omarosa. Season one's entertainingly glib cutthroat always looked out for No. 1 and wasn't afraid to dish out a little No. 2. She had a knack for finding other people's buttons and pushing them—hard. She toyed with the volatile Ereka for two episodes, brought Katrina to the brink of tears in the third, and after the Celebrity Auction paid Heidi what Trump called "the worst compliment I've ever heard" when under the pretense of singing Heidi's praises she managed to question her professionalism and class. Even Amy, who everyone agreed got along best with her, called Omarosa "a scheming, conniving bitch." Omarosa made it clear that she hadn't signed on to make friends. She seemed to believe that if she undercut the people around her she'd be the only one left standing. She was wrong. In the Art Gallery boardroom, her burned bridges came back to bite her when Trump wearied of hearing about yet another squabble, this one with Heidi over how much time to take for lunch. Ironically, Omarosa had just turned in her strongest performance of the season, and was, in fact, the only member of her team who had sold any art. It didn't matter. Omarosa had proved that she wasn't a team player, so Trump declined to invite her onto his.

"At times, Donald was down and everybody was all over him but he just hung tough, boy. He took a lot of slings and arrows of outrageous fortune, he really did. I was there with him and I know what he went through and it was tough. He'd always have a smile and he was always Donald. I loved him, I thought he was great, and I stood with him and he rewarded the friendship. He's a loyal friend."
—George Steinbrenner

CHAPTER 10

HOW TO BE
A REAL ESTATE MOGUL

If there's one thing Donald Trump knows like the back of his hand, it's real estate. He learned its ins and outs as a boy from his father, developer Fred Trump, then made his name with audacious and successful ventures in the '70s and '80s. Today, his name adorns much of Manhattan's skyline, as well as distinctive properties in many of America's distinguished zip codes. *Apprentice* applicants knew there'd be no fooling The Donald on his home turf, as it were. Omarosa couldn't even slide by after a small piece of plaster fell on her head in the Apartment Renovation episode. "All my life I've been hit on the head with plaster," snapped Trump. Here are some equally bruising—albeit emotional—lessons learned on *The Apprentice* that aspiring real estate moguls could tuck beneath their hard hats.

Recognize Potential

In the Apartment Renovation episode, Versacorp and Protégé were asked to choose which of two rundown flats they preferred to fix up and rent. The first place project managers Katrina and Troy looked at was in better shape and had a higher assessed value than the second. But real estate veteran Katrina knew that appearances could be deceiving. "It looks like an absolute disaster," she told her teammates. "However, if you have vision you could do a lot more with the second one." Katrina was right; unfortunately, it didn't do her any good: Troy overheard her telephone conversation and nabbed the promising second place for Protégé. Although Katrina moved mountains to prove her own prediction false, masterminding a major overhaul of the first apartment and persuading a contractor to refurbish both kitchen and bathroom for $1,500, Troy's team nevertheless raised their rent by a much higher percentage than Katrina's. Katrina's eye for potential had inadvertently handed the competition an insurmountable advantage.

"When you say potential, it depends on what you're looking for in the long run. Real estate takes all kinds of shapes. Does it have the potential for the type of investment you're looking to make?"
—George Ross

Don't Ask Clients to Use Their Imaginations

Raj's victory should have been assured in the Home Improvement episode—who better to lead a real estate task than a man in the business? The teams were given $20,000 with which to increase the value of comparable suburban homes. But when a contractor left a bathroom incomplete, he learned that a fixture's worth a thousand words. "Raj's game plan is good, but he made one big mistake," observed Matthew Calamari as Raj rather sheepishly showed Trump's assessors his results. "The game plan was to get a bathroom on the second floor finished, but I think that looks terrible," he said. Raj assured the judges that everything was in place and tried to get them to see beyond the work-in-progress, but even his exceptional wordsmithery wasn't up to the job. The place wasn't ready to be shown, and Raj, who had earlier admitted that the bathroom "looked like nothing," knew it. "I wish visually it looked as close as it really is," said Raj as he conducted his tour. Replied an assessor: "Me, too."

Stand Up to Contractors

- The single biggest factor in Raj's yellow taxi ride into oblivion was his passivity in the face of a contractor who overpromised and under-delivered. Raj knew that finding the right person for the job would be crucial to his team's victory. "There's nothing more common than contractors not doing things when they say they're going to do it," he cautioned early on. Sure enough, it soon became obvious that Apex had cast its lot with a loser. "I think the contractor was definitely screwing around with Raj," observed Jennifer M. as the renovation fell behind schedule. Raj needed to take decisive action: either motivate the listless men or find someone else. But Raj, for all his formidable erudition—or perhaps because of it—couldn't send a strong message when he had to. "Let us eat our tacos, we'll get back in there," yawned a worker after Raj's last-ditch appeal for speed. Naturally, the job was still unfinished when the judges arrived.

- Katrina took a lot of flak for sometimes relying on charm over substance, but her interactions with her contractor in the Apartment Renovation episode showed that the two could be synonymous. First, she secured his services for a sum that final four applicants Bill and Nick laughingly acknowledged they could never have gotten anyone to agree to. Later, when the erratic Tammy made the workers miserable, Katrina let them know that they could tell her to get lost. Unlike the diffident Raj, Katrina connected with her contractor in a relaxed, confident, and even friendly manner. The results were palpable. Bill estimated that she'd won the team $20,000 worth of work for a fraction of that figure. Katrina's deft handling of her contractor was a smashing success.

How to Recognize Potential in Residential Real Estate

Home Improvement episode judge RuthAnn Fay, a top broker associate with fourteen years experience in listing and selling properties from Manhattan to Montauk Point, shares tips for sizing up that new home.

There are five basic fundamentals for recognizing potential in any residential property.

- **Location**
  The old saying still holds true: "Location, location, location." Where the property is situated is always the first priority. Be sure to find out what its proximity is to industry, highways, shopping, and schools. If it's good, you're on the right track.

- **Foundation**
  Any structure is built on a foundation; if this is determined to be sound, everything else can usually be fixed. So make sure your foundation is a sturdy one.

- **Condition**
  When you walk into a property for the first time, the condition is usually determined right away. If you can see that it's a mess, then it is. How much of a mess is the question. Ask yourself "Is this original condition?" "Original" usually pertains to the age of the property. If you are in a home that is forty years old, does the kitchen, for instance, look the same? Start calculating immediately. Do your homework on the cost of materials.

- **Size**
  The amount of space you have to work with is always a factor. Square footage, the number of bedrooms and bathrooms—these can greatly determine a high or low value in any home.

- **Resale**
  Ask yourself, "Who would this property appeal to if I were to sell it?" This is a very important step in recognizing potential. It is always valuable to know in advance who your buyers might be, such as singles coming out of a rental or perhaps a couple with one or two children. Start to think this way and spotting potential will be as easy as 1, 2, 3, 4, 5.

How to Make the Most of a $20,000 Renovation Budget

RuthAnn Fay reveals how to make every dollar count.

- **The Renovation Determination**
  The first thing to do is assess the condition of the entire property. Look specifically at kitchens and bathrooms. These are two of the biggest sources of value in a home. If they need to be renovated, do it.

- **The Kitchen**
  After the location factor, the kitchen is one of the strongest selling points in any home. A new kitchen is a focal point, a conversation area, and often the most used room in the house. I would allot $10,000 of my budget and start there.

- **The Bathrooms**
  Depending on how many baths your home has, you can usually get away with putting in a new bath for approximately $5,000. Raj should have focused and completed both bathrooms. I would definitely have finished the job and simply cleaned the remainder of the house.

- **Cosmetic Cleanup**
  Plantings and shrubbery outside a home can create great curb appeal. This can be done at minimal cost and usually looks high-quality. Sometimes a simple coat of paint or a good cleanup in a home can go a long way. You would be surprised just how far.

Four Minus One Equals Failure

Raj committed a second major real estate no-no in the Home Improvement episode when he turned a four-bedroom house into a three-bedroom house. His teammates looked askance when their project manager told them to tear down a wall, but Raj could not be deterred. Viewers got the sneaking suspicion that it was the thrill of demolition that motivated Raj as much as his developer's instincts, but of course the man himself put it in more philosophical terms: "There's nothing more consistent in human nature than both the desire to destroy and to create. We're destroying and we're creating. This makes Raj happy." Far less happy was Donald J. Trump, who was furious about more than Raj talking about himself in the third person. "He made a big mistake," said The Donald. "He took a four-bedroom house and he made it into a three-bedroom house. Even if the bedrooms are a little bit larger, I'd rather be selling a four-bedroom than a three-bedroom." Trump's appraisers agreed, and the loss was the end of the line for *The Apprentice*'s most recondite applicant.

The holes in Raj's renovation plan are even larger than the one in the bedroom wall.

Look out below! As their deadline looms, Apex makes tracks—all over the carpet and lawn.

Little Things Mean a Lot

If God is in the details, Apex made a pact with the Devil in the Home Improvement episode when they tumbled ass over tea kettle out of the house. Equipment was tossed from second-story windows and paint was spilled on the lawn. Whatever advantage the team gained by working until the buzzer was more than offset by the mess they left behind. While Raj labored mightily to call attention to his crew's attractive renovations, Trump's assessors instead marveled at the shortsightedness of installing new carpet only to let it be destroyed by mud and paint. Raj would have been better served by trading in some of his grand plans for a bucket of soapy water and a tarp.

"Many times you hear the expression that God is in the details. When people come in to buy something, especially very rich people, they see details. If something's wrong they see it, and it reflects on the price. That's why I'm up early in the morning to check every detail of my construction sites. It's a little bit like watching somebody sell their used car and not wash it. You can spend ten dollars washing the car and get another two hundred dollars for the car. I've seen guys selling cars that are dirty, and I say that guy is a loser."

—Donald Trump

CHAPTER 11

TIME MANAGEMENT

"*Time is money.*"
—Donald Trump

Every minute counted on *The Apprentice*. Teams had to perform overnight miracles: transform a vacant storefront into an inviting eatery; invent an office product that even Staples hadn't thought of; design a new clothing line from scratch. Tasks that would ordinarily take weeks got crammed into a few short hours. Teams could fall irrevocably behind in a few squandered seconds. Sleep was scarce and sometimes nonexistent. It was a brutally efficient way to weed out anyone who was unprepared to do things at Trump speed—and it taught viewers how to make the most of precious time.

Finish What You Start

"My game plan really was to treat this like a football game," said project manager Sam at the start of the Buying Low episode. From the Versacorp ranks he named a cheerleader, kicker, quarterback, and coach, ordered them onto the "field," then went upstairs to start calling plays. It soon became clear that Sam was no business-world Vince Lombardi. When Nick gave him the (incorrect) information that gold is best purchased early in the day, Sam ordered his team to drop everything and go buy bullion. Unfortunately, that command came with Bill, Kwame, and Bowie poised to buy several items from the team's shopping list at rock-bottom prices in Chinatown. A morning's work was lost and the team wound up paying top dollar for those same items as time ran out. After Protégé consequently kicked Versacorp through the uprights for the third straight task, Trump cut Sam from the team.

Catch the Competition Napping

Amy's ten consecutive victories must have worn her out; when the big guy bused the teams to Atlantic City for their Casino competition, she fell sound asleep like the rest of Versacorp. Meanwhile, the back of the bus buzzed with activity as Troy, Kwame, and Bill planned their attack. "The whole time on the bus we're just talking strategies, game plans, we're making appointments," Troy observed. "I look up at the other team and they're all sleeping. Every single one of them [is] sleeping like this is a tour-guided bus. This is a job interview!" Protégé hit the boardwalk running, while Versacorp played catch-up all episode long. Amy looked atypically off balance and rolled snake eyes for the first time in season one. Versacorp's wise use of early minutes ensured that they'd hit the jackpot later on.

Don't Be Hamlet

- Wes's sluggishness took a steep toll on Mosaic in the Doggie Business episode when a search for a charity partner kept the team's "extreme dog makeover" business in the kennel during the crucial lunchtime rush. Whatever gains were made by donating proceeds to Kitty Kind ("A pretty bad

"On occasion I go to some other cities and it's like the Middle Ages. Things aren't up-to-date. I went down to Texas once, I got off the plane at 10:30 and the guy says 'Come on we'll have a drink.' I'm ready to get back on the plane and go finish my work after a half hour and I gotta drink and have lunch before we even sit and talk."

—George Ross

charity with respect to dogs," noted Trump) were more than offset by the two hours lost in the hunt. Most dog walkers had hung up their leashes by the time Wes ordered his crew onto the field. "I thought that [Wes] was a little slow in some decision-making," reported Kelly in the boardroom—a big problem in a task that had to happen fast.

- The consequences were clear when Danny beat his breast rather than make a decision in the Nescafé Taster's Choice episode. Stephanie had found Magna an event planner to run their promotional extravaganza, but the price would eat up most of the budget. Danny just couldn't bring himself to make such a high-stakes choice. So Magna stewed while their leader paced. By the time Danny—at Alex's urging—mustered the stones to close the deal, he had to pay whatever the planner asked. His negotiating room had vanished with the hours. Worse, the team was left with a terribly narrow window in which to develop a promotional plan—if Bren hadn't thought up an iPod giveaway, the team might have been stuck with Michael's European models and guys in coffee-cup suits. Trump later showed how to make a good decision quickly when he sent Magna's colorful but hesitant leader down to the street.

Find That Fifth Gear

Mosaic's capacity for fast, furious, focused action won the day when they took Kevin's eleventh-hour Ciao Bella flavor idea—Donut Ice Cream—and literally ran with it! The Apex women had come up with an obscure flavor—Red Velvet—but one that could be created from the ice-cream factory's in-house ingredients, while Mosaic's doughnuts had to come from outside suppliers. With the factory deadline mere minutes away, team Mosaic couldn't hesitate for a second. They piled into their van and descended like locusts on every doughnut shop they could find. "We jump out of the van like the A-Team, go running into this poor Dunkin' Donuts, push all these people aside," said Pamela, describing the squad's MO. "Put 'em in the bag and no one gets hurt," joked Chris as cashiers cowered and children wailed. When the Mosaic van screeched to a stop back at the factory, they had their ingredients—and the satisfaction of knowing they'd taken Kevin's idea from the conference room to the doughnut stores to the factory floor . . . all in under half an hour!

"Ideally, you want quick decision-makers. However, you can't make it so quick that the decision's going to be wrong. I'd rather have somebody take their time and come out with the right decision, but the best combination is good decision-making, quickly."

—Donald Trump

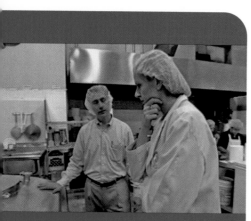

I scream, you scream . . . for Pam to quit asking questions!

Too much contemplation of canine couture wrapped up the win for the competition.

Bedeviled by Details

"Go! Hut, hut, hut, hut!" Pamela kept things moving during Mosaic's wild doughnut ride, but her quarterbacking might not have been necessary if she'd kept an eye on the clock earlier in the day. During the team's tour of Ciao Bella's ice-cream factory, Pamela developed an insatiable appetite—for knowledge. All of a sudden no production detail was too small. "Pamela takes the dime tour as if we're in Disneyland, and starts asking a thousand different questions about how ice cream is made," Andy complained Pamela's thoroughness was misplaced in a sales task "I don't give a damn what the rotator splint on a boiler does," said Andy. "I'm here to sell ice cream."

Don't Waste Time on Bad Ideas

Wes should have pulled the plug right away on Stacy R.'s dead-end doggie dress-up idea in the Doggie Business episode. He sensed right away that her plan to buy outfits and sell photos of "Western Dog," "Girlie Dog," and "Bad-Ass Dog" was unreasonable. "It just didn't make any sense from a cost-recovery standpoint," he said. Yet Wes accompanied Stacy on a trip to a pet store to price out the costumes that he already knew were too expensive. In a task where every second counted, spending time on Stacy's bad idea was a big mistake. Wes should have found a way to bring his quarrelsome teammate in line without bringing the entire team down.

Carolyn's Time Management Tips

1. Surround yourself with extremely good people.

2. Choose your spouse very carefully.

Silence the Bigmouth

- Wes's inability to cut off a loquacious team member's chatter finally undid him in the Levi's Catalogue episode. Throughout season two, Maria had shown a lot of passion—and an inability to channel it productively. Project managers who gave her what Andy called "finite guidelines" found her to be a major asset. But Wes found himself steamrolled. First Maria usurped his authority when he tried to hurry the photo shoot along and Mosaic nearly missed its deadline. Worse, Wes later let a fight between Maria and Sandy over Maria's editing-room power grab rage on and on while the time for their presentation to Levi's executives loomed. Naturally, Maria ran roughshod over the presentation too, while the rest of the team, its nominal leader included, squirmed. Some of them hadn't even had time to find Levi's jeans to wear! "He cannot control the troops," said Bill Rancic as Wes's boardroom doom closed in. "They had a major fight go on for thirty minutes in their war room and Wes sat back and watched the entire thing." Wes had let one too many prolix partners turn his team into a rudderless ship. As Tara would note in season three: If you're fighting, you're not working.

- Bren showed that he had the right stuff when he cut Stephanie's tirades short in the Business on Wheels episode. Stephanie was, in Bren's words, "full of piss and vinegar" when Bren ordered her, Erin, and Michael to deliver cheeseburgers from Manhattan to the rest of the team in Queens. But Bren had no appetite for the negativity that arrived with his food. When Stephanie demanded to know why Bren hadn't arranged for third-party delivery, Bren shut her down hard. "Don't sit there and sling [bleep]," he said. "These things you're criticizing you could've taken care of yourself." He gave a repeat performance in the boardroom when he stifled Stephanie's criticism with a counterattack so determined that it almost got her fired. Trump was impressed, and Bren was never in serious danger. He'd silenced the bigmouth—and showed that he had a leader's voice.

"I was once asked the difference between business and government, and I said, 'Business is a dog-eat-dog world—and government is just the opposite.'"

—Michael Bloomberg

CHAPTER 12

NAILING THE INTERVIEW

Although the interview is always the second-to-last episode, it's actually the first step in snagging a job. The best *Apprentice* candidates got a chance to put their best feet forward—or in their mouths—when they were put through the wringer by the business world's best. Guest stars like New England Patriots owner Robert Kraft, Bear Stearns legend Alan "Ace" Greenberg, Pepsi prez Dawn Hudson, and Domino's Pizza chief David Brandon mercilessly grilled the *Apprentice* elite in grueling interviews. The applicants' answers revealed their characters—and a host of interview dos and don'ts for us to remember.

DO: Know the Organization

Sandy and Jennifer M. finished season two's interviews in a dead heat. Jennifer M.'s Princeton and Harvard pedigree was impeccable, but Sandy's real-world entrepreneurial success also impressed. When the two went head-to-head before The Donald, Sandy stumbled when challenged to name the number of employees in the Trump Organization. Jennifer knew the number, and broke the tie.

DON'T: Try to Change It

Asked by Trump Chief Financial Officer Allen Weisselberg what he'd do on his first day on the job, Nick replied that he'd "present a vision for the organization." Weisselberg was incredulous. "And you'll be able to do that on day one without even knowing the first thing about this entity?" he queried. Nick looked grim; he knew he'd overreached. Get your foot in the door before trying to change the locks.

"Honesty. Integrity. And I'd say a spark of creativity or enthusiasm. Those are all qualities which I would look for."

— George Ross on What He Looks for When He Hires

DO: Prepare Answers

Craig's wide-eyed, deer-in-the-headlights double takes and vague replies made him seem caught off guard by question after question. Pressed for details, he couldn't come up with any. Craig's failure to rehearse answers to even the most predictable inquiries (i.e., "What's the most challenging business problem you ever faced and how did you handle it?") made him look unprepared—and unfit for the finale.

DON'T: Use Them Inappropriately

Amy's well-practiced assessment of her value to the Trump Organization might have been music to Acquisitions Chief Charley Reiss's ears—if he'd asked her about it. But his request ("I'd like to hear your description of the organization") had nothing to do with Amy's value, and her attempt to divert the discussion made her look like a slick politician rather than a qualified candidate. "Amy kind of reminded me of a Stepford wife," Charley later told the boss. "Her answers were basically meaningless." Amy had memorized her lines but delivered them at the wrong time.

DO: Include the Unexpected

"Within fifteen minutes I was dead bored with talking to her," said Charley Reiss after Amy's "empty" answers turned him off. No such complaint was heard from Prudential Douglas Elliman's Real Estate Chairman Howard Lorber when Kendra answered his skepticism by threatening to compete with Trump if he didn't hire her. Lorber liked Kendra's moxie—enough to make her his No. 1 one choice in the boardroom.

DON'T: Forget to Expect It

Season one winner Bill wasn't easy to rattle, but Trump International Hotel and Tower G.M. Tom Downing did his best. "Obviously you've been getting by on your instincts," he told the Loyola grad. "[You're] sure as hell not getting by on your education." Rather than let Tom's broadside get him down, Bill calmly stood his ground and declared himself proud of his schooling. His confidence in fending off an ambush let the interviewer know he'd found the right man.

DO: Be Likable

Kwame answered tough questions about his energy level with an easy smile and a disarming rapport. Even executives who felt ambivalent about his qualifications thought his manner made him worth another look. Said Tom Downing: "He's got a likability about him, and in my business if you can get an extra two or three minutes out of somebody when you're sitting face-to-face with them because you're likable, that's important."

DON'T: Be Slick

Nick gave his interviewers a dose of the assertive confidence that made him a great copier salesman and a Trump favorite. But when Tom Downing asked, "What are you going to bring to the table other than your charisma?" there wasn't much Nick could say. "He's a little bit too slick for his own good," Tom told Trump. "I honestly didn't walk away from that meeting feeling like I know him." Shiny surfaces don't impress executives who look beneath them.

"Be honest. I'd rather have a person of integrity with fewer credentials than someone full of hot air with great credentials."
—Donald Trump

DO: Let Them See the Real You

"You just have to be yourself," said Tana before showing viewers how to do just that, making it personal right away with a story about her entrepreneurial mother's inspiring example. By the time she left Darlene Daggett's office, the QVC executive knew the profit margin on Tana's first business venture as a 9-year-old well enough to repeat it in the boardroom. Tana was open about her life as a wife, mother, and businessperson, and most interviewers were smitten. "I was Tana," she shrugged. That was enough.

DON'T: Hide Every Flaw

It's the oldest interview question in the book: what are your weaknesses? When Trump executive Norma Foerderer put this chestnut to Bill in his season one interview, the future Apprentice dodged with the tried-and-true: "I'm never satisfied." But Norma wasn't born yesterday. "That's not a weakness," she said as Bill scrambled for another answer. By trying to hide every imperfection, Bill revealed things he never meant to. Which was probably the question's real purpose all along.

The First Thing Madeline Devries Looks For

I have to think they're nice. I have to like them. Now that's not why I would hire someone, but that's the first thing that comes to mind. Can I live with that person? Can I be in meetings with them? Can I talk to them? Do I want my clients to be with them? Is this someone who fits into our culture?

DO: Map a Life Plan

Law school. Business school. Professional football. His own software company. Season two's Kevin seemed to have it all—except a clear sense of where he was headed. The experts agreed that he succeeded at whatever he set his mind to. But Pepsi's Dawn Hudson noted that his life seemed to be a series of "course corrections," and she wondered if after joining the Trump Organization he might change course again. Kevin lacked direction, so The Donald directed him to the street.

DON'T: Forget the Company's Place in It

Craig could speak at length about past jobs, but not the one for which he was applying. He built a strong case for himself as a candidate—for another company. Howard Lorber pointed out that Craig actually wanted to change the Trump Organization in order to fit him in. When he couldn't explain how his experience had prepared him for a job with Trump, interviewers realized it hadn't.

"I want to know why they left their last job. And if they give me a casual answer like 'Well, I wasn't making enough money' or 'The company got downsized' or 'I decided I want to try something else'—that to me doesn't score well. If, on the other hand, they say 'Well, I couldn't stand my boss's guts,' that shows a certain ability on their part to expose their character. That, to me, is good."

—George's Favorite
Interview Question

Miscellaneous Questions

- Tell me about your leadership style—what's it like to work for you?
- Would you enjoy working for you?
- When is it appropriate to bend the rules?
- What do you think would be your ideal job in the Trump Organization?
- How important is education to you?
- Do you consider yourself a loyal employee?
- Who is on your enemy list?
- Why should Donald Trump hire you for this job?

"I have no interest whatsoever in first impressions. That's nonsense. I'm interested in what his friends and co-workers think of him and what his clients think of him. Anybody can con you in an interview. Now if a guy comes in and he smells and needs a shave that's something else, but assuming they look presentable I pay no attention to them."

—"Ace" Greenberg on Interviews

CHAPTER 13

HOW TO SURVIVE IN THE BOARDROOM

Boardroom rivals battled to the end in most *Apprentice* episodes. From time to time, Trump let an applicant know that he or she was safe, but usually the atmosphere was thick with suspense. Anyone could go. As in the tasks themselves, one move could make the difference between winning and losing. But which was the right move? Was it time to speak up or pipe down? Was it time to point fingers or acknowledge mistakes? Applicants with bad boardroom instincts learned where they'd gone wrong; when The Donald pulled the trigger he always explained why. By season three, he must have been sick of repeating the following:

Know When to Shut Up

If there was one lesson that applicants couldn't seem to grasp, it was this: loose lips sink ships. (Maybe it was because so many of them were lawyers or salesman who made money with their mouths.) No matter how many candidates dug their own graves by flapping their gums out of turn, another motor mouth inevitably did the same thing a week or two later. The boardroom table needed a plaque that read, "Quit while you're ahead." At least once per season, a career-ending case of logorrhea reminded viewers that silence can be golden.

"Erin, if you keep talking you might get fired, but at this moment you're probably not. Go ahead, keep talking. Go ahead."

—Donald Trump

Tammy overshares.

Bradford misjudges his invincibility.

Season One

Trump barely noticed Tammy after the Apartment Renovation task. She stood in the back while Katrina complained to Trump about Troy's unscrupulous (according to Katrina) behavior. Troy had gained the upper hand at the beginning of the task by writing "I want exactly what you want" on the slip of paper on which he was supposed to reveal which apartment he wanted. Defeat did nothing to cool Katrina's anger. She vehemently denied that she'd been duped and her team backed her up. "I've been duped many times," Trump admitted. "Everyone's duped." Still, Versacorp presented a united front in Katrina's defense. United, that is, until a voice chimed in from the back. "I think we got duped, to be honest," said Tammy, her internal editor characteristically out to lunch. Her teammates were furious, and Trump was not impressed. "Your disloyalty has been just terrible," he said as he let Tammy go. With one ill-considered comment, Tammy brought herself out of the margins and into Trump's crosshairs.

Season Two

Bradford was at the top of his game in the Ciao Bella episode. He'd distinguished himself by volunteering to take charge of Apex for the Child's Play task, won a boardroom exemption by piloting them to victory, and turned in the team's strongest performance during their losing effort to sell the most ice cream in Times Square. So confident was he of his position that he gave up his exemption and faced the music along with his teammates. It seemed like a smart and safe way to build camaraderie—until the music Bradford faced became his funeral dirge. "Bradford made a stupid, impulsive, life-threatening decision that, frankly, if you were running a company and made that kind of a decision you'd destroy that company instantaneously," said Trump when he fired the guy who moments ago had been the season's front-runner. Bradford seemed like a guy who might go all the way, but a slip of the lip led to a very big fall.

Season Three

Michael fancied himself a favorite with the ladies—and with Trump. "The only thing separating me and Donald Trump is a few billion dollars," he trumpeted at the start of the Business on Wheels episode. "I think we're the same people." "Michael's a jackass and he's nothing like Donald Trump," retorted Erin, proving that Michael was wrong about the ladies. Was he wrong about Trump, too? We found out at the end of the episode when Michael went into the boardroom as the overwhelming favorite for firing. He'd been a miserable massage salesman and his abysmal track record had made him, again in Erin's words, "a boardroom cliché." But losing project manager Bren unexpectedly gave Michael a reprieve when he suggested that Trump fire Stephanie instead. Surprised, Trump forgot about Michael and watched his two teammates tangle. But Michael just couldn't keep his mouth shut. He took potshots at Bren until, predictably, he shot himself in the foot. "[Bren]'s knocking the hell out of Stephanie . . . and you're interrupting him with nonsense," said the incredulous Trump. "I mean, how stupid can you be?" Soon a yellow taxi separated Michael still farther from Donald Trump.

Michael decides to participate at exactly the wrong time.

Kwame's quiet helped usher Omarosa out the door.

John zipped his lip and let Audrey talk her way out of a job.

In contrast, these applicants made clear the value of knowing when to curb one's tongue:

- The Art Gallery episode could have been the end of the line for Kwame. Protégé had taken a royal beating, and the team's weakest member, Omarosa, had worked harder and smarter than ever before. The buck seemed likely to stop with the project manager. But in the boardroom Kwame sat back and let Heidi and Omarosa slug it out until Trump wanted nothing more than for the bickering and excuse-making to stop. He cut Omarosa loose, and Kwame ran with his second chance all the way to the finale.

- John G. talked smack about project manager Audrey throughout the Miniature Golf task, so viewers braced for a titanic clash when she pulled him before Trump after Net Worth's loss. But in the boardroom, the big man with the big mouth unexpectedly quieted. He knew that he'd already given Audrey enough rope to hang herself. Sure enough, she lashed out indiscriminately and with enough vitriol to turn off even Angie, her sole supporter. John looked dignified in comparison, a gently disapproving grown-up who, unknown to Trump, had hours before called names like a vicious schoolboy.

> *"Branson went after me, I killed him. Cuban went after me, I killed him."*
>
> —Donald Trump on Rival Reality-Show Billionaires

> *"When somebody's stepping on your toes, you better learn how to scream."*
>
> —George Ross

Fight Back

Trump respected applicants who understood when it was time to kill. He wanted to know that his future Apprentice was strong enough to take whatever the rough-and-tumble New York business world dished out. Boardroom punching bags always took a coup de grâce from the boss. Applicants who gave better than they got usually lived to see another task.

Jessie's Girl

Kristi's indecisive leadership left her vulnerable in the Flea Market episode's aftermath, but it was her "friend" Jessie who really did her in. Jessie advised Kristi to stay quiet in front of Trump no matter what, and that's exactly what Kristi did—even after Jessie turned against her and said that she should be fired. Jessie may have started off with the best intentions; the emotional Kristi could easily have crumbled during a dirty boardroom brouhaha. But under The Donald's demanding gaze, Jessie threw Kristi to the wolves and Kristi took it like a lamb. "Kristi, until tonight you were a star," Trump said. "But then I saw Heidi fighting for her life, I saw Omarosa fighting for her life, and I didn't see that fight in you. . . . You never even said anything in your own defense, and I don't get it." Finally Kristi got the message and tried to argue, but it was too late. After she'd gone, trusted Trump employee Bernie Diamond illustrated the importance of fighting back. "She took the heat without any defense," he said, "which meant it was all true."

Control the Conversation

Sandy proved that a wild verbal torrent can turn the tide when she beat back a coordinated assault from Andy and Jennifer M. in the Pepsi Edge episode's boardroom. Sandy's teammates had conspired to scapegoat her after Pepsi's judges mauled Mosaic's barbell bottle, and the bridal salon owner looked like a goner for sure. She'd stumbled her way through the task's presentation and the candidates making a case against her were an elite lawyer and a Harvard debate champ. But Sandy came off the ropes swinging. She couldn't refute her opponents' charges, so she simply drowned them out. She got passionate. She got loud. Even a Harvard debate champ can't do much if he can't get a word in edgewise. Finally Trump ended the bloodbath. Sandy had TKO'd Andy with her relentless attack. She hadn't made a case for herself as anything other than a fighter, but in Trump's eyes that was plenty.

Kristi took careful notes as Jessie scripted her epitaph.

Sell Your Ideas

In the Doggie Business episode, Raj's perseverance helped Apex come out on top after project manager Jennifer M. dismissed his suggestion that they open a second location. A lot of candidates would have stewed, content to lose, and then point fingers in the boardroom. But Raj stuck to his guns. He politely but firmly presented his idea again when revenues stayed flat. Jennifer eventually listened, and the team's expansion worked beautifully.

On the other team, Stacy R. offered one I-told-you-so too many when she blamed their loss on Wes's failure to heed her ideas. Trump noted that he'd heard this from Stacy before. Time and again, she'd thrown her hands up when others didn't immediately recognize her brilliance. The Donald pointed out that the best brainstorm in the world has no value if you can't express it persuasively. "You can't just say 'This is an idea I have and take it or leave it,'" he said. "You have to sell the idea."

> *"If you think an idea is really good, then just don't stop. Go after it. Keep selling it. 'Cause some of the greatest ideas were ideas that nobody wanted."*
>
> –Donald Trump

> *"Unusual appearance could certainly create a specific impression, but in a major organization like the Trump Organization that doesn't work. It's the wrong way. Don't stick out. Anyone who goes with a cane when you don't need it and wears bow ties and two-tone shoes, you're creating a particular impression of a personality, but if the personality is not consistent with the business environment you're looking to go into—why?"*
>
> —George Ross

The Clothes Make the Man

Raj turned heads when he made his first appearance in a bow tie and red pants. His sartorial splendor set him apart before he even opened his mouth (that's when things really got unusual). At first, Raj's outrageous outfit appeared to be a mistake. Andy compared him to Rodney Dangerfield and other candidates reacted to him as if he was wearing clown suit to the prom (sweet-talking the ladies with Stalin references didn't help, either). When Raj added a cane to the ensemble it seemed like one affectation too many. "What are you carrying the cane for?" demanded The Donald. "You look like you have two very good legs to me." Later, however, we all realized how clever Raj had been. When Trump dined with the victorious Apex team after their

Child's Play triumph, what he wanted to talk about was Raj! "So what's with the guy with the cane?" he asked, more interested in the colorful character who'd caught his eye than in the humdrum details of Apex's win.

Before hurrying off to your haberdasher, recall Danny's fate. Like Raj, he made his debut in unconventional togs. But in Danny's case the reactions to his burnt orange leisure suit were decidedly, well, bittersweet. In the boardroom, Donald asked whether someone who dressed like Danny was suited for the Trump Organization and his teammates, concerned about their own fates, were only too happy to pile on. Danny survived, but when we saw him again he'd traded in his downscale look for a traditional business suit. It's good to stand out—just make sure it's for the right reason.

The other competitors smirked, but Raj's fashion sense intrigued Mr. Trump.

Danny's work duds worked The Donald's nerves. Unbelievable!

CHAPTER 14

YOU'RE FIRED!

"Losing's a bitch." —Donald Trump

There were no losers on *The Apprentice*. Each candidate was chosen from a pool of hundreds of thousands—if not millions—of applicants. Prime-time television exposure made them famous in their fields and offered a springboard from which to launch new real-world ventures. Still, there was plenty of emotion every time Donald Trump pointed his finger and spoke those two awful words. Ferocious competitors to the last, cast members never wanted to be the one to take that walk of shame from the elevator to the waiting yellow taxi. They'd planned, pleaded, bullied, BSed, gone without sleep, worked their tails off, and thrown their hearts and souls into winning. Elsewhere in life that is almost always enough. But on *The Apprentice*, for all but one applicant each season there would come that fatal error—that irretrievable moment when a wrong choice spelled disaster. Here's a look at those self-inflicted mortal wounds and the rules that might have made a difference.

Season One

Lemonade Stand

Fatal error: David's energy overpowers his intellect when he chases customers so aggressively that they flee.

Chapter 6: Not All Salespeople Are Created Equal

Marquis Jet

Fatal error: Jason decides that meeting with clients is a waste of time and the women prove him dead wrong.

Chapter 6: Know Your Customer

Buying Low

Fatal error: Sam wastes a morning's work when he orders his team out of Chinatown before they get anything done.

Chapter 11: Finish What You Start

Planet Hollywood

Fatal error: Versacorp's pitchmen are a hit in Times Square, but Bowie drops the ball at the merchandise counter once diners come inside.

Chapter 6: Don't Walk Away Once the Customer's in the Door

Flea Market

Fatal error: Kristi stays put at her indoor table when clearing skies draw customers outside.

Chapter 1: Location, Location, Location

Celebrity Auction

Fatal error: Jessie doesn't change her tune even when her pitch affects Isaac Mizrahi like fingernails on a chalkboard.

Chapter 3: Read the Client's Cues

Apartment Renovation

Fatal error: In the boardroom, Tammy stands out in the wrong way when she sides with the competition's project manager rather than with her own.

Chapter 13: Know When to Shut Up

"It's always hard to fire people. It's always hard, but sometimes it has to be done. It goes with the territory. If somebody doesn't do their job you got to get rid of them. You try to do it as humanely as possible. But if people plead for a job you got to be firm, you got to tell them like it is."

—George Ross

Trump Ice

Fatal error: Ereka lets her feelings get the better of her when she melts down in front of Carolyn.

Chapter 8: Control Your Emotions

Art Gallery

Fatal error: Omarosa sows discord for the last time when she tangles with Heidi over how much time to take for lunch.

Chapter 9: Address Personal Conflicts Before They Spill Over

Pedicab Fleet

Fatal error: Trump tires of hearing Heidi lay blame at everyone's feet but her own.

Chapter 8: Watch Your Mouth!

Casino

Fatal error: Instead of attacking the task with both barrels, Katrina hangs back hoping to see Amy fail.

Chapter 8: Celebrate Your Colleagues' Strengths

Penthouse Rental

Fatal error: Troy's effort to start a bidding war backfires when he pushes too hard and a customer walks out.

Chapter 6: Sometimes It's a Mistake to Do the Hustle

Interviews

Fatal error: During the interviews, Nick needs more than a too-smooth pitch to sell himself.

Chapter 12: DON'T: Be Slick

Fatal error: Amy's interviewers get their backs up when her answers don't fit their questions.

Chapter 12: DON'T: Use Prepared Answers Inappropriately

Finale/Golf Tournament/Jessica Simpson Concert

Fatal error: Kwame fails to fire a liar, so Trump turns to Bill instead.

Chapter 7: Demand Loyalty

> *"Evaluating the quality of your staff is an ongoing process and it's never easy. At some point you're going to have to get rid of your weakest link."*
>
> –Donald Trump

Season Two

Child's Play

Fatal error: Rob doesn't know that eels lack appendages—or that sometimes you have to blow your own horn.

Chapter 5: Assert Yourself

Ciao Bella

Fatal error: Bradford waives his immunity to show he's one of the gals, so Trump shows him the door.

Chapter 13: Know When to Shut Up

Vanilla Mint Crest

Fatal error: Stacie J. consults a Magic 8 Ball instead of convincing her teammates that she's someone they want to keep around.

Chapter 11: Distinguish Yourself on Day One

Restaurant Opening

Fatal error: Jennifer C.'s mouth works harder than the rest of her as she sets an unruly example for a dispirited squad.

Chapter 8: Walk the Talk

QVC TV

Fatal error: Pamela decides that it's better to be feared than to be loved when she takes over Apex, so when the team goes under, the life raft leaves without her.

Chapter 7: How to Take Charge of a New Team

Fashion Show

Fatal error: Project manager John fails to act when his staff sets price randomly—and too high.

Chapter 6: Know When to Shoot for the Moon on Price

Doggie Business

Fatal error: When Wes ignores her ideas, Stacy R. simmers instead of selling them.

Chapter 13: Sell Your Ideas

"I find it extremely difficult, particularly if a person's been here for a while, and I'll do everything I can to save them. I think it's good for morale if they know you have concern for people and their lives."

—"Ace" Greenberg on Firing

NYPD Recruitment

Fatal error: Elizabeth backs down when her team demands a militaristic recruitment campaign.

Chapter 8: Stand Your Ground

Home Improvement

Fatal error: Raj lets his lazy contractor walk all over him—and the brand-new carpet!

Chapter 10: Stand Up to Contractors

Bridal Shop

Fatal error: Chris creates a self-fulfilling prophecy when he pronounces the task impossible.

Chapter 8: Set a Positive Tone

Levi's Catalogue

Fatal error: Wes gives away Kelly, the only team member who might have kept Maria from running wild.

Chapter 7: Don't Fear Talent

Pepsi Edge

Fatal error: Andy dulls the Edge with a barbell-shaped bottle and geography-themed wrapper.

Chapter 4: Find the Right Packaging

M-Azing Bar

Fatal error: Ivana may as well raise a white flag along with her skirt when too much eye candy obscures the client's candy.

Chapter 6: It's All About the Product

Interviews/Polo Cup/Basketball Classic

Fatal error: Kevin's work experience is all over the place, so Trump tells him to keep looking.

Chapter 12: DO: Map a Life Plan

Fatal error: When Sandy can't name the number of employees in the Trump Organization, she ensures that she won't be added to it.

Chapter 12: DO: Know the Organization

Finale/Polo Cup/Basketball Classic

Fatal error: Jennifer M. refuses to own up to her errors, while Kelly takes his lumps—and the victory.

Chapter 8: Be Accountable

> *"If you feel somebody should go, they go, and you don't have to explain why. Explaining only makes you weaker as a leader."*
>
> —George Ross

Season Three

Burger King

Fatal error: Todd collects his thoughts instead of making sure Alex trains enough cashiers.

Chapter 8: Prioritize

Motel Hell

Fatal error: Brian sinks so much of his budget into toilets that Net Worth has nothing left for beds.

Chapter 5: Don't Waste Waste

Nescafé Taster's Choice

Fatal error: Danny calls a vote when it's time for a big decision, so Trump calls him a cab.

Chapter 7: The Case for Dictatorship

Dove Cool Moisture

Fatal error: Kristen and Erin end their brainstorming sessions before finding ideas that work.

Chapter 2: Wait for the Big One

Business on Wheels

Fatal error: When Bren attacks Stephanie in the boardroom, Michael pipes up instead of lying low.

Chapter 13: Know When to Shut Up

Graffiti Billboard

Fatal error: Tara marries her own idea before hearing what the client has to say.

Chapter 6: Listen Up!

Miniature Golf

Fatal error: Audrey blows a chance to mend fences with John G. and gets blown away in the boardroom.

Chapter 9: Address Personal Conflicts Before They Spill Over

Musician Experience

Fatal error: John G. negotiates for what he knows he can get instead of pushing for more.

Chapter 3: Read the Client's Cues

Home Depot

Fatal error: Erin jokes about her disinterest in the project but, in the boardroom, The Donald doesn't think it's funny.

Chapter 5: Turn A No-Win into a Big Win

Domino's Pizza

Fatal error: Stephanie obsesses over getting a handful of pies to Brooklyn while the competition buries her with a handful of high-volume customers.

Chapter 6: Find the Buyer Who Can Buy the Most and You Won't Have to Find the Most Buyers

American Eagle Outfitters

Fatal error: Angie chokes when Net Worth arrives disorganized and late for its presentation.

Chapter 5: Harmonize

Pontiac Solstice

Fatal error: Chris signs off on dull text while his opponents appeal to emotion.

Chapter 6: Aim for the Heart

Staples

Fatal error: Bren bares his risk aversion in the boardroom.

Chapter 5: What's Life Without a Little Risk?

Hanes T-Shirt

Fatal error: Alex fails to fight for more focus on promotion when Tana drags him to Staten Island in search of a Bedazzler.

Chapter 8: Prioritize

Interviews/Video Game Championship/Athlete Challenge

Fatal error: Craig's garbled responses make him the interviewers' least favored candidate.

Chapter 12: DO: Prepare Answers

Finale/Video Game Championship/Athlete Challenge

Fatal error: Tana badmouths her bigmouths too often for Trump's taste, while Kendra's respect for her team wins her the job.

Chapter 5: Crunch Time Counts the Most

"You have to love what you do. You can never give up. You can never quit. You can never ever quit."

–Donald Trump

CHAPTER 15

THE EPISODE SYNOPSES

SEASON ONE

"Women have a tougher time in the workplace, or so they say," declared Mr. Trump when he divided the teams by gender at the start of season one. "Let's find out." We found out, all right: the women wiped out half the men's squad in four straight episodes, and had a lot of fun doing it. Everyone was shocked except The Donald. "I've always said women are tougher than men," he'd later say. "This proves it."

Every viewer could find someone to root for. There was Troy, the self-made charmer from Boise, Idaho, who proved he was the equal of his better-educated competitors by outlasting almost all of them; Amy, Austin's golden girl, whose ten-task winning streak made her the one to beat; the brilliant, laid-back Kwame, who never let us see him sweat; Heidi, who won us over with her salty tongue and combative spirit; Nick, the copier salesman with confidence to spare; and Bill, the methodical Chicago cigar aficionado who, right from the start, had the air of a winner. There was

comic relief from Sam, an Internet entrepreneur, who might be found in the foyer exercising in his underwear. There was even a villain: Omarosa Manigault-Stallworth, who left a Godzilla-size trail of emotional wreckage in her wake and betrayed the only applicant who believed in her in the season's finale.

If watching *The Apprentice* was like cramming an MBA into thirteen weeks, we couldn't have asked for better classmates.

Lemonade Stand

Task: Sell lemonade on the streets of New York.

Winning Team: Protégé
Ereka (project manager), Amy, Heidi, Jessie, Katrina, Kristi, Omarosa, Tammy

Losing Team: Versacorp
Troy (project manager), Bill, Bowie, David, Jason, Kwame, Nick, Sam

While the quarrelsome Protégé women get off to a slow start, Versacorp hits the ground running. However, the men's organization and aggressive—in David's case too aggressive—sales tactics don't amount to much when foot traffic at their seaport location dries up. Meanwhile the women dole out kisses and phone numbers at a well populated midtown spot and sell lemonade for $5 a cup. Sam's Hail Mary bid to sell a single cup for $1,000 fails, and Versacorp pays Trump's boardroom its inaugural visit.

Reward: A visit to The Donald's luxurious Trump Tower apartment
Boardroom: Troy, David, Sam
Fired: David

Marquis Jet

Task: Create an ad campaign for the Marquis Jet Card.

Winning Team: Protégé
Amy (project manager), Ereka, Heidi, Jessie, Katrina, Kristi, Omarosa, Tammy

Losing Team: Versacorp
Jason (project manager), Bill, Bowie, Kwame, Nick, Sam, Troy

After legendary adman Donnie Deutsch gives them their marching orders, Amy and Ereka sit down with Marquis Jet executives while Jason decides that such a meeting would be a waste of time. The men work hard—except for Sam, who takes a nap—and turn in a solid but uninspired effort, while the squabbling women win big with a daring campaign that capitalizes on the Marquis Jet's phallic shape.

Reward: An elegant dinner in Boston
Boardroom: Jason, Nick, Sam
Fired: Jason

> *"I think being fired is just a learning experience. It only makes you that much more knowledgeable and that much stronger and gives you more of a desire to succeed."*
>
> – Carolyn Kepcher

Buying Low

Task: Negotiate lower-than-retail prices for miscellaneous items.

Winning Team: Protégé
Jessie (project manager), Amy, Ereka, Heidi, Katrina, Kristi, Omarosa, Tammy

Losing Team: Versacorp
Sam (project manager), Bill, Bowie, Kwame, Nick, Troy

Sam stages a suite-doorway sit-in after no one welcomes him back from the board-room, and the women are once again at one another's throats. But Protégé is all business out on the streets as the women flirt, beg, and even dance their way to substantial discounts. Meanwhile Sam feeds his field team incorrect information and orders them out of Chinatown before they can pick up the items they need. Troy endures his first (he says) leg wax, but his sacrifice is in vain. The women win again.

Reward: Dinner at the famous 21 Club
Boardroom: Sam, Kwame, Bowie
Fired: Sam

Planet Hollywood

Task: Manage one night's shift at Times Square tourist hotspot Planet Hollywood.

Winning Team: Protégé
Katrina (project manager), Amy, Ereka, Heidi, Jessie, Kristi, Omarosa, Tammy

Losing Team: Versacorp
Kwame (project manager), Bill, Bowie, Nick, Troy

It's a party at Planet Hollywood when the Protégé women tug on tight T-shirts and make themselves the restaurant's main attraction. The "Shooter Girls" ring up strong alcohol sales and lift a glass or two themselves. The more sober-minded men focus their efforts outdoors, where Troy appalls Nick by passing Kwame off as a celebrity in order to move merchandise. Inside, things are quiet despite Bill's well-received staff cash incentives. Trump tempers the women's joy at their fourth straight triumph by warning against relying too much on sex appeal to win.

Reward: A trip to Trump National Golf Club
Boardroom: Kwame, Bowie, Nick
Fired: Bowie

Flea Market

Task: Purchase and resell items at a flea market.

Winning Team: Versacorp
Nick (project manager), Amy, Bill, Ereka, Katrina, Tammy

Losing Team: Protégé
Kristi (project manager), Heidi, Jessie, Kwame, Omarosa, Troy

A corporate reshuffle mixes the women with the few remaining men, and Nick is only too happy to let the ladies do his leading for him. Kristi's indecisiveness keeps her team out late picking products, but when rain falls on market day her indoor table seems like the place to be. However, when the sun peeks out, Protégé's sales evaporate and Versacorp's custom shirts fly off the rack. It's a boardroom whodunit when more than $100 vanishes somewhere between Omarosa's hand and Kristi's back pocket, but it's Jessie's bad advice that does Protégé's leader in.

Reward: Meet George Steinbrenner at Yankee Stadium

Boardroom: Kristi, Heidi, Omarosa

Fired: Kristi

Celebrity Auction

Task: Create a personal experience with five celebrities for a charity auction.

Winning Team: Versacorp
Bill (project manager), Amy, Ereka, Katrina, Nick, Tammy

Losing Team: Protégé
Omarosa (project manager), Heidi, Jessie, Kwame, Troy

Versacorp negotiates experiences with Regis Philbin, Rocco DiSpirito (*The Restaurant*), Carson Daly, Tiki Barber (New York Giants), and Ed Bernero (Executive Producer, *Third Watch*) despite Tammy's mouth, which goes off like a badly aimed bazooka. Troy's deal-making drawl saves Protégé time and again during meetings with Russell Simmons, Kate White (Editor, *Cosmopolitan*), Nicole Miller (fashion designer), *Queer Eye*'s Fab Five, and Isaac Mizrahi (fashion designer), and the latter is so relieved to get away from Jessie's monotone that he gives Troy a hug. At Sotheby's, the bids break Versacorp's way.

Reward: None—the teammates went out for a night of drinking and dancing on their own

Boardroom: Omarosa, Heidi, Jessie

Fired: Jessie

Apartment Renovation

Task: Renovate and rent a run-down apartment.

Winning Team: Protégé
Troy (project manager), Amy, Heidi, Kwame, Omarosa

Losing Team: Versacorp
Katrina (project manager), Bill, Ereka, Nick, Tammy

Omarosa gets plastered when a small piece of drywall crowns her at a Trump construction site. Troy tricks real estate whiz Katrina into revealing which apartment has more potential, then enrages her further by winning a coin flip to claim it. Katrina's revenge seems certain when she oversees a whiz-bang renovation, but a lack of prospects dooms Bill's efforts to secure a high rent for Versacorp's apartment. In the boardroom, Tammy forgets to put the safety on her mouth and deepens Trump's scowl lines when she sides with Troy over her own project manager.

Reward: A picnic at the palatial Trump home in Bedford, New York

Boardroom: Katrina, Bill, Tammy

Fired: Tammy

Trump Ice

Task: Distribute Trump Ice spring water.

Winning Team: Protégé
Heidi (project manager), Amy, Kwame, Omarosa, Troy

Losing Team: Versacorp
Ereka (project manager), Bill, Katrina, Nick

Both sides field fractious sales teams as Versacorp's Ereka tunes out Bill's ideas and Protégé's Amy kicks Omarosa under the table. Nick refuses Ereka's order to research customers online and then embarrasses himself the next day with a graceless pitch. Troy proves that there's substance behind his smile when he overcomes merchants' storage problems with just-in-time deliveries, and Ereka breaks down in front of Carolyn when the team's paperwork is in shambles at the deadline. Kwame and Troy cement their friendship at the gym, while Amy and Nick cement their navels on the dance floor.

Reward: An aerial tour of Manhattan from Trump's private helicopter

Boardroom: Ereka, Bill, Nick

Fired: Ereka

Art Gallery

Task: Sell an emerging artist's work at a gallery.

Winning Team: Versacorp
Nick (project manager), Amy, Bill, Katrina

Losing Team: Protégé
Kwame (project manager), Heidi, Omarosa, Troy

Nick trusts his gut and chooses the accessible artist Andrei's work, while Kwame and company cast their lot with their artist Meghan's high-priced but disturbing creations. Omarosa and Heidi have an R-rated blowout over whether or not to sit down for lunch. Unless Heidi planned to squeeze an art appreciation class into that time slot, it doesn't make a difference. At Protégé's disastrous gallery show, Heidi mistakes Meghan's fireplace cover for a toilet tank and that's exactly where Protégé's fortunes go. Omarosa shows vulnerability while waiting to meet with Trump in the boardroom, but it's too late: Trump sends her packing.

Reward: A ten-minute private meeting with Trump in his apartment
Boardroom: Kwame, Heidi, Omarosa
Fired: Omarosa

Pedicab Fleet

Task: Manage one shift of a pedicab company.

Winning Team: Versacorp
Bill (project manager), Amy, Katrina, Nick

Losing Team: Protégé
Troy (project manager), Heidi, Kwame

Bill's brainstorming session brings out the best in Amy, who comes up with the idea to sell advertising on the team's vehicles, and the worst in Katrina, who throws a fit when she feels she's valued more for her body than her brain. Troy's brainchild—prepaid ride cards—goes nowhere with New Yorkers and team morale nosedives when a Versacorp cab rolls by with an ad on the back. Although Troy drums up business by putting on his cowboy hat and having fun in the driver's seat, it's too little too late. Versacorp leaves tire marks all over Protégé.

Reward: A private yacht tour of New York Harbor
Boardroom: Troy, Heidi
Fired: Heidi

Casino

Task: Execute a promotional plan to register gamblers at the Trump Taj Mahal Hotel and Casino in Atlantic City.

Winning Team: Protégé
Kwame (project manager), Bill, Troy

Losing Team: Versacorp
Amy (project manager), Katrina, Nick

Protégé gets the jump on the competition by planning on the bus while Versacorp naps. Kwame's team thinks big and assembles a promotional event that includes a huge gambling wheel, a $1,000 giveaway, dancers, and a white tiger. More important, Bill negotiates the exclusive right to escort VIP gamblers from their special check-in line at the hotel to Protégé's promotional table. Meanwhile, Versacorp offers its registrants a chance to win a $300 car rental and spends the rest of the time trying to poach Protégé's players with sexy models and a louder bullhorn. Amy's ten-task winning streak finally ends, but her stellar record keeps her on Trump's good side—for now.

Reward: $1,000 gambling money and a night in the Taj's finest penthouse

Boardroom: Amy, Katrina

Fired: Katrina

Penthouse Rental

Task: Lease the Trump World Tower's penthouse for an evening.

Winning Team: Versacorp
Nick (project manager), Amy

Losing Team: Protégé
Troy (project manager), Bill, Kwame

Nick and Amy laugh off Trump's ribbing about their rumored relationship, but once the task is under way there's nothing to smile about. Amy doesn't like Nick's talky salesmanship and neither of them like their lack of customers. Protégé fares better with several prospects, but Troy's pressure tactics turn off one of the most promising. A last-minute lessee tips the task to Versacorp, and Nick's father and Amy's sister join the winners for their reward.

Reward: A flight in Trump's private jet to his opulent Florida club, Mar-a-Lago

Boardroom: Troy, Kwame

Fired: Troy

Interviews

Task: Interview with four high level Trump employees.

The final four–Amy, Bill, Kwame, and Nick—endure a grueling series of interviews with Trump employees Norma Foerderer (Vice President, Media Relations & Human Resources), Alan Weisselberg (Chief Financial Officer), Charley Reiss (Head of Acquisitions), and Tom Downing (General Manager, Trump International Hotel and Tower). Their general consensus is that Nick is a salesman and little else, and that Amy gets on everyone's nerves. Both are fired. (Continued . . .)

Boardroom: Amy, Bill, Kwame, Nick
Fired: Nick, Amy

Finale/ Golf Tournament/ Jessica Simpson Concert

Task: Take charge of a special event.
Golf Tournament Team: Bill (project manager), Amy, Katrina, Nick
Jessica Simpson Concert Team: Kwame (project manager), Heidi, Omarosa, Troy

Bill is assigned to run the Chrysler Trump Golf Tournament, and Kwame is put in charge of a Jessica Simpson concert at the Taj Mahal. Offered the services of six recently fired candidates, Bill picks Amy, Katrina, and Nick, while Kwame chooses Troy, Omarosa, and Heidi. Bill's crew runs afoul of Leslie Rey, Trump National Golf Club's Director of Sales and Events, when they cram her office full of boxes. Omarosa ignores orders from Diane, the Taj's Entertainment Coordinator, to confirm Jessica Simpson's travel arrangements and consequently, loses the music star entirely. Kwame realizes he's been lied to, but keeps Omarosa on his team.

Jessica Simpson makes her way to the Taj Mahal on her own and puts Kwame's team back on track . . . but not for long. No one tells the kitchen when to bring the star's breakfast, no one tells the hotel staff that the meet and greet needs a bigger room, and no one tells Troy to butt out when he horns in on Heidi's turf. No one should have to tell Omarosa to stay put when she hears that The Donald is on his way to meet Jessica, but she escorts the

singer away and refuses to answer her phone, stranding Kwame with an increasingly irate billionaire. Meanwhile, Bill's ass is frozen grass when a frost delay threatens the Chrysler Trump Golf Tournament. While waiting for warmth, Bill's teammates ask him to chill; his maniacal energy's driving them nuts. But his mad pace comes in handy when he rescues a sponsor's missing sign mere seconds before its executives arrive. In season one's final boardroom, Kwame's failure to reel in Omarosa makes the difference in a tight race. Bill Rancic is the Apprentice!

Boardroom: Bill, Kwame
Hired: Bill

SEASON TWO

This time eighteen applicants gathered for fifteen weeks of hell. Trump once again split them by gender, but he also added a twist: project managers who led their teams to victories were exempt from being fired the following week.

Season one's cast was a tough act to follow, but the new crew had its share of standouts: Jennifer M., the lethal blond beauty who cruised beneath the radar until her sprint to the finish; Sandy, a feisty bridal salon owner who never backed down from a fight; former Army intelligence officer Kelly, whose military precision and strategic thinking made him a double threat; Andy, the Harvard debate champ who couldn't seem to win his opponents' respect even as he took them out one by one; the underrated Ivana, whose stinging boardroom ripostes made even The Donald wince; and Raj, whose bow tie and cane let everyone know that he's his own man.

Child's Play

Task: Develop a new toy for Mattel.

Winning Team: Apex
Bradford (project manager), Elizabeth, Ivana, Jennifer C., Jennifer M., Maria, Sandy, Stacie J., Stacy R.

Losing Team: Mosaic
Pamela (project manager), Andy, Chris R., John W., Kelly, Kevin, Raj, Rob, Wes

Bradford and Pamela cross gender lines to lead the teams. Rob can't keep up during Mosaic's brainstorming session, and over at Apex, Bradford rams his own idea down the women's throats. However, when his pitch makes Mattel executives frown, Bradford changes his tune. The women's "Metamorphor" hits it big with a children's focus group, while Mosaic's "Crustacean Nation" is shellacked. Stacie J. unnerves her teammates when she looks into a Magic 8 Ball and it apparently says "Act crazy."

Reward: Dinner with Donald and Melania in their palatial Trump Tower apartment

Boardroom: Pamela, Andy, Rob

Fired: Rob

Ciao Bella

Task: Develop and sell a new ice cream flavor.

Winning Team: Mosaic
Kelly (project manager), Andy, Chris R., John W., Kevin, Pamela, Raj, Wes

Losing Team: Apex
Ivana (project manager), Bradford, Elizabeth, Jennifer C., Jennifer M., Maria, Sandy, Stacie J., Stacy R.

Neither Kelly's "G.I. Joe mode" nor Ivana's wishy-washy leadership produces flavor ideas until the very last minute. The men burn rubber to buy their Donut Ice Cream's ingredients in time, while the women decide that Red Velvet sounds hot, which it does, especially when Jennifer M. says it. Concerned that their attractive female competitors will outsell them on the street—especially after they help themselves to Mosaic's marketing plan, which the men have left in plain sight—Kelly's team sells with gusto, while the women are disorganized and restrained. When Apex standout Bradford waives his boardroom exemption in a gesture of solidarity, Trump unexpectedly gives him the gesture that goes with the words "you're fired."

Reward: A meal at caviar wonderland Petrossian

Boardroom: Ivana, Bradford, Jennifer C., Stacie J.

Fired: Bradford

Vanilla Mint Crest

Task: Create buzz about Procter & Gamble's new toothpaste.

Winning Team: Mosaic
Kevin (project manager), Andy, Chris R., John, Kelly, Pamela, Raj, Wes

Losing Team: Apex
Elizabeth (project manager), Ivana, Jennifer C., Jennifer M., Maria, Sandy, Stacie J., Stacy R.

After legal worries sink Andy's idea to give away a chance to win $1 million, the team bounces back with a promotional circus that banks on fun rather than money. Meanwhile, the women are sitting pretty after New York Mets superstar Mike Piazza brushes his teeth at their event, but Maria's failure to watch the bottom line puts Apex over budget and in the boardroom. Stacie J.'s wacky 8 Ball episode comes back to haunt her as Trump releases her onto the streets of New York City.

Reward: Dinner aboard the *Queen Mary 2*
Boardroom: Elizabeth, Maria, Stacie J.
Fired: Stacie J.

Restaurant Opening

Task: Open a restaurant and earn the higher Zagat ratings for food, service, and decor.

Winning Team: Mosaic
Raj (project manager), Andy, Chris R., John W., Kelly, Kevin, Pamela, Wes

Losing Team: Apex
Jennifer C. (project manager), Elizabeth, Ivana, Jennifer M., Maria, Sandy, Stacy R.

Under Jennifer C.'s chaotic leadership the women offer sleepy service, while the men do whatever it takes—including sending John out to preen for appreciative customers—to show their customers a good time. Jennifer's post-loss rant against "old Jewish bat ladies" takes her feud with Stacy to a new level, and it's Jennifer who comes out on the losing end when they settle their differences in the boardroom.

Reward: A meeting with former New York City mayor Rudy Giuliani
Boardroom: Jennifer C., Elizabeth, Stacy R.
Fired: Jennifer C.

QVC TV

Task: Pick, price, and sell a product on live TV.

Winning Team: Mosaic
Chris R. (project manager), Andy, John W., Kelly, Kevin, Raj, Wes

Losing Team: Apex
Pamela (project manager), Elizabeth, Ivana, Jennifer M., Maria, Sandy, Stacy R.

Trump orders Pamela to move over to Apex and bring home a win for her fellow females, but her hardnosed style leaves her friendless when overpricing brings the team down despite Jennifer M.'s telegenic salesmanship. Meanwhile, Kelly hits the bull's-eye with his high price point, but Pamela's high price keeps customers—and her chances for becoming the Apprentice—away.

Reward: Tennis with John McEnroe and Anna Kournikova at Arthur Ashe Stadium

Boardroom: Pamela, Maria, Stacy R.

Fired: Pamela

Fashion Show

Task: Present a new fashion line at the Avon Fall Fashion Show.

Winning Team: Apex
Maria (project manager), Elizabeth, Ivana, Jennifer M., Sandy, Stacy R.

Losing Team: Mosaic
John W. (project manager), Andy, Chris R., Kelly, Kevin, Raj, Wes

Even the women's persistent infighting can't derail them this time around as the men wander through the task like children who desperately want to leave the department store. Kelly tries to change their course by seizing the reins and even the designer's pencil, but to no avail. John W. blows off pricing responsibility and the men finally go down.

Reward: Invitations to a private celebrity party

Boardroom: John W., Andy, Kevin

Fired: John W.

Doggie Business

Task: Create a dog service business.

Winning Team: Apex
Jennifer M. (project manager), Chris R., Elizabeth, Ivana, Kevin, Raj

Losing Team: Mosaic
Wes (project manager), Andy, Kelly, Maria, Sandy, Stacy R.

New teammates sniff each other out after a corporate reshuffle remixes the packs, but they might have saved their breath: nothing reveals character faster than holding a pit bull's head while your partner trims its nails. Apex gets down and dirty with multiple locations and gleefully degrading services like dog massages, while Mosaic plays dead with a late start and unimaginative ideas. Andy leaves himself vulnerable after he answers charges of immaturity by leaving the team's cell phone in a taxi, but Trump has a bigger bone to pick with Stacy, whose refusal to take responsibility leaves her sticking her head out the window of a yellow taxi.

Reward: A meeting with New York City mayor Michael Bloomberg

Boardroom: Wes, Andy, Stacy R.

Fired: Stacy R.

NYPD Recruitment

Task: Develop a recruitment campaign for the New York City Police Department.

Winning Team: Mosaic
Andy (project manager), Kelly, Maria, Sandy, Wes

Losing Team: Apex
Elizabeth (project manager), Chris R., Ivana, Jennifer M., Kevin, Raj

Andy finally answers his critics with a heartfelt campaign and tenacious leadership that never wavers despite his teammates' aggressive second-guesses. In contrast, Apex teeters on the lip of insurrection as Elizabeth sways back and forth between her team's demands for a militaristic theme and her own, softer vision. When she withdraws her support for Kevin's promising eleventh-hour brainstorm, she loses her last ally and twists in the wind for the rest of the task—and in the boardroom.

Reward: A viewing of the winning TV ad on Times Square's jumbo screen

Boardroom: None—Elizabeth summarily fired

Fired: Elizabeth

Home Improvement

Task: Increase a house's assessed value for under $20,000.

Winning Team: Mosaic
Sandy (project manager), Andy, Kelly, Maria, Wes

Losing Team: Apex
Raj (project manager), Chris R., Ivana, Jennifer M., Kevin

The season's first four fired contestants return to the scene of their crimes for one task only and either redeem themselves with hard work, like Bradford and Rob, or sow more dissension, like Stacie J. and Jennifer C. Apparently still feeling his oats from the previous episode, Andy takes charge when Mosaic's contractor falters and invites a crew of "goodfellas" to come in and get things done. Elsewhere, Raj leads Apex blindly with confidence, unwisely knocking out a wall to reduce the home's number of bedrooms while his unsupervised contractor puts his feet up. When Trump's assessors arrive, the job isn't finished, but Raj is.

Reward: A helicopter ride to Denise Rich's incredible Hamptons home

Boardroom: Raj, Ivana, Kevin

Fired: Raj

Bridal Shop

Task: Transform an empty space into a bridal shop for an exclusive sale.

Winning Team: Mosaic
Kelly (project manager), Andy, Maria, Sandy, Wes

Losing Team: Apex
Chris R. (project manager), Ivana, Jennifer M., Kevin.

With bridal salon owner Sandy in the ranks, Mosaic is the prohibitive favorite this time around. Sandy and project manager Kelly don't let overconfidence kill them, however, and they attack the task like underdogs. Maria's botched e-mail blast—correctable once Sandy catches it—is the only bump in Mosaic's road to victory. Meanwhile, tough Chris R.'s face falls the moment he hears the assignment and he's a dead man walking all episode long.

Reward: $50,000 of merchandise from Graff Jewelers

Boardroom: Chris R., Ivana, Kevin

Fired: Chris R.

Levi's Catalogue

Task: Develop an in-store promotional catalogue for Levi's.

Winning Team: Apex
Kevin (project manager), Ivana, Jennifer M., Kelly

Losing Team: Mosaic
Wes (project manager), Andy, Maria, Sandy

Wes starts out on the wrong foot by sending Kelly to Apex, and Mosaic's a mess thereafter. Diva Maria runs out the clock with a studio tantrum and a twenty-minute conference room quarrel, and the team presents to Levi's in another company's jeans. Elsewhere, the Apex hotties shake their own moneymakers for the cameras, and prove that they're more than just pretty faces by inventing an innovative "fit wheel" to showcase Levi's' wares. Jennifer M.'s teammates take potshots at her like planes buzzing King Kong atop the Empire State Building, and Kevin practically sweats Rorschach ink blots onto his shirt during the presentation, but Apex's combination of butts and brains is good enough to win.

Reward: A private tour of the set of Billy Joel's Broadway play *Movin' Out,* led by the composer himself

Boardroom: Wes, Andy, Maria, Sandy

Fired: Maria, Wes

Pepsi Edge

Task: Design a brand-new bottle and marketing campaign for Pepsi's newest product.

Winning Team: Apex
Kelly (project manager), Ivana, Kevin

Losing Team: Mosaic
Andy (project manager), Jennifer M., Sandy

Andy helps himself to a bit too much of the client's product and leads like an overexcited schoolboy, choosing a geography theme for Mosaic's bottle and marketing campaign and waving cash incentives at Pepsi's designers even as he refuses to let them eat. With the smell of pizza wafting past the hungry group's nostrils while a 23-year-old Harvard man hops around waving greenbacks, it's a wonder no one beats Andy to death with his barbell-shaped bottle. Over at Apex, the only hole in Kelly's plan is the one he leaves through the *D* in Apex's bottle, which spells out the product's name in bold letters. Andy's caffeine buzz has worn off by the time Mosaic hits the boardroom, and the debating champ's listless defense before Sandy's onslaught earns him the elevator ride to the street.

Reward: The chance to race Lamborghini Gallardos

Boardroom: Andy, Jennifer M., Sandy

Fired: Andy

M-Azing Bar

Task: Personally make and sell M&M/Mars's new candy bar.

Winning Team: Mosaic
Sandy (project manager), Jennifer M.

Losing Team: Apex
Ivana (project manager), Kelly, Kevin

Former enemies Sandy and Jennifer M. make up and take down Apex with eye-catching, hormone-releasing outfits and shameless street solicitation that nets them $5 a bar and a chance of being snared in an NYPD vice-squad sweep. With Kelly seemingly coasting on his exemption and Kevin making unauthorized price cuts, Ivana makes a desperate bid for victory and *The Apprentice*'s most popular screen capture by dropping her skirt for whoever ponies up $20. And, oh yeah, they get a chocolate bar. In the boardroom, George gives her kudos, but The Donald is unforgiving. Ivana exits with her internationally exposed tail between her legs.

Reward: A day with Bill Rancic in Chicago
Boardroom: Ivana, Kelly, Kevin
Fired: Ivana

Interviews/Polo Cup/ Basketball Classic

Task: Interview with four business luminaries. Take charge of a special event.

Polo cup team: Kelly (project manager), Elizabeth, John W., Raj

Basketball classic team: Jennifer M. (project manager), Chris R., Pamela, Stacy R.

Season two's interviewers are Alan Jope (COO, Unilever HPC, North America), Dawn Hudson (President, Pepsi Cola, North America), Alan "Ace" Greenberg (Chairman, Executive Committee, Bear-Stearns), and Robert Kraft (Owner, New England Patriots). The group pronounces Kevin bright but directionless, and Sandy likable but unprepared for the corporate world. Both are fired. Kelly takes on the Genworth/Trump Polo Cup with a talented staff that doesn't like him all that much and quickly micromanages their enthusiasm away. Jennifer goes the other way, delegating some of the Genworth Charity Basketball Classic's most important assignments to Pamela, who's only too happy to take over. Kelly ponders his fate when he learns that he has to scramble to prepare for a Tony Bennett performance and rain threatens to wash out the entire event. Jennifer likewise has lots to think about when sponsors question her preparedness and emcee Chris Webber cancels. (Continued . . .)

Boardroom: Jennifer M., Kelly, Kevin, Sandy
Fired: Kevin, Sandy

Finale/Polo Cup/ Basketball Classic

Task: Take charge of a special event.

Polo Cup Team: Kelly (project manager), Elizabeth, John W., Raj

Basketball Classic Team: Jennifer M. (project manager), Chris R., Pamela, Stacy R.

Both Jennifer and Kelly prove adept at putting out fires, which is a good thing because there are a lot of them. Jennifer replaces Chris Webber with NBA Commissioner David Stern, tries again to reassure her anxious sponsors, and finds generators after a power outage kills the basketball players' Xboxes. Meanwhile, Kelly mediates an argument between Elizabeth and Raj and has to find an acceptable alternative when he learns that a sponsor's logo can't be spray-painted in the goals as promised. The Basketball Classic goes well, although Pamela looks more like the one in charge than the largely invisible Jennifer, and The Donald is left unattended after the game to walk bemusedly back to his helicopter. Kelly, on the other hand, makes sure Mr. Trump has everything he needs—except a clean chair to sit on. After the match, Kelly and company race to tidy the disgusting clubhouse for Tony Bennett and finish the job in the nick of time. Afterward, it's Jennifer's fire versus Kelly's efficiency in the season's final boardroom.

Trump turns to a live audience for advice, and the overwhelming choice is Kelly. Trump is eventually convinced, and it is official: Kelly Perdew is the Apprentice. We get a final replay of Ivana in her underwear, and with that, season two is over.

Boardroom: Jennifer M., Kelly
Hired: Kelly

SEASON THREE

This time it's Book Smarts versus Street Smarts when Trump divides the group between those who have college degrees and those without. Season three's indelible competitors included: Bren, the pint-size boardroom terror who couldn't decide whether he should have left Tennessee; Danny, the "morale officer" who preferred a guitar to a business suit; Kendra, who lay low for weeks before revealing herself as an indefatigable front-runner; Craig, a proud papa whose garbled communication almost obscured his surefire instincts; Erin, a former beauty queen and current man-eater with the balls to throw Trump a wink; the volatile Chris, whose wild outbursts were the product of an outsized heart; Alex, the boyish wonder who burned brightly then burned out; and Tana, the sunny Iowa mom who knew when to hang back and when to hit the competition hard.

Burger King

Task: Choose a new burger to market and sell.

Winning Team: Net Worth
John G. (project manager), Angie, Audrey, Brian, Chris S., Craig, Kristen, Tana, Tara

Losing Team: Magna
Todd (project manager), Alex, Bren, Danny, Erin, Kendra, Michael, Stephanie, Verna

Trump needles the Magna Book Smarts by telling them that their opponents earn three times more than they do. Some of the Net Worth Street Smarts look as if they might have trouble following The Donald's math, but hey, they can afford accountants. Both teams undergo crash training courses at separate Burger King franchises, and right off the bat we establish that the *Apprentice*'s gain is not necessarily the service industry's loss. A dog pees on Tana—seriously—when she picks up plane tickets from a broker, but otherwise it's smooth sailing for Net Worth. Not so at Magna, where Danny's "horrific" promotion isn't even the team's biggest problem. Trump punishes Todd for not training enough people for the registers and/or for being the least weird character in the bunch.

Reward: Dinner with Donald and Melania in the 21 Club's secret basement dining room

Boardroom: Todd, Alex, Danny

Fired: Todd

Motel Hell

Task: Renovate a motel on the Jersey shore for $20,000.

Winning Team: Magna
Michael (project manager), Alex, Bren, Danny, Erin, Kendra, Stephanie, Verna

Losing Team: Net Worth
Brian (project manager), Angie, Audrey, Chris S., Craig, John G., Kristen, Tana, Tara

Each team finds itself assigned to an outwardly nice-looking motel that turns out to be a dilapidated house of horrors inside. In both cases, a knuckleheaded male P.M. runs afoul of his female budget director: Kristen rips Brian a new one when he spends money without a budget and goes broke before buying new beds, while Michael accuses Verna of handling the money because she doesn't want to handle a paintbrush. Magna's customers join them for a late-night party around the pool (maybe to get away from the paint fumes in the rooms), whereas Net Worth's customers wonder whether to call 911 when Brian and Kristen have an 11 P.M. shouting match in the courtyard. Unhinged with exhaustion, Verna packs her bag and begins to walk the earth like Kwai Chang Caine in *Kung Fu* until Carolyn persuades her to return. Later, Brian tells Trump to fire him, proving that college is, if nothing else, a good place to practice making excuses.

Reward: A yacht trip with Steve Forbes, Editor-in-Chief of *Forbes* magazine

Boardroom: None—Brian summarily fired

Fired: Brian

Nescafé Taster's Choice

Task: Develop and execute a marketing campaign for Nestlé's premium coffee brand.

Winning Team: Net Worth
Angie (project manager), Audrey, Chris S., Craig, John G., Kristen, Tana, Tara

Losing Team: Magna
Danny (project manager), Alex, Bren, Erin, Kendra, Michael, Stephanie

Verna does Brian one better and actually fires herself, packing up and leaving for good before the next task even begins. Secure in his exemption, Michael daydreams aloud about marketing plans that involve European models and barks at anyone who tries to get him to actually work. Danny can't make a decision, and Magna spins its wheels until Bren brainstorms an iPod giveaway. Meanwhile, Angie suggests that Net Worth go with a patriotic election theme and her teammates agree, if only to get her to stop marching around the conference room. When the votes are tallied, Net Worth is the victor. Magna tries to get Trump to void Michael's exemption and dump him, but The Donald plays by the rules.

Reward: A nighttime helicopter ride around Manhattan

Boardroom: Danny, Michael, Stephanie

Quit: Verna

Fired: Danny

Dove Cool Moisture

Task: Make an industry-quality 30-second TV commercial for body wash.

Winning Team: None

Losing Team(s):

Magna: Erin (project manager), Alex, Bren, Kendra, Michael, Stephanie

Net Worth: Kristen (project manager), Angie, Audrey, Chris S., Craig, John G., Tana, Tara

Both teams turn in ads that could raise even The Donald's hair after Erin and Kristen go with ideas they can't pull off. Magna attempts a gag meant for the *Will & Grace* crowd but turns in something that looks like it belongs at the scene of a Paul Reubens arrest. Net Worth blows what should have been an easy joke about body wash powering a marathon runner to victory and instead delivers a repulsive mess that includes the cheesiest video effects since the heyday of *The Buggles*. Donnie Deutsch can't pick a winner, but Trump can pick a loser: Kristen.

Reward: None

Boardroom: Erin, Bren, Michael; Kristen, Audrey, Tana

Fired: Kristen

Business on Wheels

Task: Create a mobile service business in an Airstream trailer.

Winning Team: Net Worth
Tana (project manager), Angie, Audrey, Chris S., Craig, John G., Tara

Losing Team: Magna
Bren (project manager), Alex, Erin, Kendra, Michael, Stephanie

While recounting her boardroom battle with Kristen, Audrey decisively dethrones Heidi as the owner of *The Apprentice*'s filthiest mouth. Adorable mouth, but filthy. Net Worth once again beats Magna with a more creative idea by rolling out an open casting service for aspiring actors while the Book Smarts settle for an unexciting mobile spa. Michael balks at offering massages to men and his lackluster salesmanship earns him an overdue ticket to the street.

Reward: $20,000 to buy Mikimoto pearl jewelry

Boardroom: Bren, Michael, Stephanie

Fired: Michael

Grafitti Billboard

Task: Use graffiti art to create an ad for the new PS2 game Gran Tourismo 4.

Winning Team: Magna
Alex (project manager), Bren, Erin, Kendra, Stephanie

Losing Team: Net Worth
Tara (project manager), Angie, Audrey, Chris S., Craig, John G., Tana

Tara's preoccupation with showing respect for the surrounding Harlem neighborhood steers Net Worth's ad for a racing game down a creative cul-de-sac. Team members, PlayStation executives and Trump observer Jill Cremer all warn Tara that appealing to the game's target market is job number one, but she pursues her own vision to its inevitable conclusion. Losing a task aimed at the hip urban demographic to square Alex proves to be a bad omen: Net Worth never wins again.

Reward: Portraits taken by famous photographer Patrick Demarchelier

Boardroom: Tara, Craig, Audrey

Fired: Tara

Miniature Golf

Task: Build and manage a miniature golf course.

Winning Team: Magna
Stephanie (project manager), Alex, Bren, Erin, Kendra

Losing Team: Net Worth
Audrey (project manager), Angie, Chris S., Craig, John G., Tana

Tired of taking her teammates' flak, Audrey talks about her tragic childhood and the hardships that beautiful people endure. John G.'s response—that Audrey's looks will take her farther than any of them—is balanced on the border between flattery and condescension and only makes things worse. Both teams build child-friendly courses, but something's out of place at Net Worth: the huge wad of chewing tobacco in Chris's mouth. Kendra's exclusive cross-promotion with nearby Chelsea Piers makes the difference as discount flyers draw families to Magna. In the boardroom, Audrey points fingers everywhere, so Trump points his at her.

Reward: Golf with Cristie Kerr at Trump National Golf Club
Boardroom: Audrey, Angie, Craig, John G.
Fired: Audrey

Musician Experience

Task: Negotiate a personal experience with five music industry artists to be auctioned off during a live FUSE TV broadcast.

Winning Team: Magna
Kendra (project manager), Alex, Bren, Craig, Tana

Losing Team: Net Worth
Chris S. (project manager), Angie, Erin, John G., Stephanie

After Trump mixes the Book Smarts with the Street Smarts, John G. heads off with Erin and Stephanie to make deals with Barenaked Ladies, Gene Simmons, New Found Glory, Simple Plan, and Fat Joe. John cuts the women off whenever they try to speak, which is too bad, because the musicians don't seem all that crazy about him or his humdrum ideas. Even when Gene Simmons says he wants his experience to attract the evening's biggest bid, John fails to set his sights higher. Magna's negotiators—Tana and Craig—ask for more from Lil' Jon, Eve, Jadakiss, Lil' Kim, and Moby—and get it. On the air, Tana surprises everyone with her straight-out-of-Compton vocabulary and the "playaz in the hizzy" respond with strong bids for Magna's special experiences. Even though Erin proves to be a natural in front of the camera and keeps her composure with Gene Simmons's finger in her ear, Net Worth comes in a distant second thanks to John's lousy deals.

Reward: None
Boardroom: Chris S., Erin, John G.
Fired: John G.

Home Depot

Task: Put on an in-store do-it-yourself construction clinic.

Winning Team: Magna
Craig (project manager), Alex, Bren, Kendra, Tana

Losing Team: Net Worth
Angie (project manager), Chris S., Erin, Stephanie

Craig's executive decision to do a clinic about building and decorating a box bores his teammates, but they eventually promise their best efforts when he asks for them. Thinking inside the box pays off for a change when Magna's event turns out to be fun for adults and children alike. On the Net Worth side, Erin can barely figure out which end of a hammer to hold, while her exasperated teammates look as if they'd like to plant one in her head. However, it turns out that no one on the team is exactly handy when their mobile kitchen cabinet assembly clinic turns into a time-consuming comedy of errors. In the boardroom, Erin throws Trump one wink too many and is sent packing.

Reward: A chance to experience weightlessness during a flight in a specially outfitted 727

Boardroom: Angie, Erin, Chris S.

Fired: Erin

Domino's Pizza

Task: Create a new pizza and sell it from a mobile kitchen.

Winning Team: Magna
Bren (project manager), Craig, Kendra, Tana

Losing Team: Net Worth
Stephanie (project manager), Alex, Angie, Chris S.

When The Donald admits a fondness for meatballs, both teams know exactly what they want on their new pies. Tana and Kendra sew up the task for Magna before it's really begun by taking orders from nearby businesses. Net Worth's truck is nearly the site of the most one-sided fistfight since the Louis–Schmeling rematch when simple pie man Chris takes exception to Alex's nonstop flirting with female customers. There's plenty of blame to go around in the boardroom, but Stephanie's decision to personally deliver pizzas to Brooklyn proves to be the blunder that bothers Trump the most.

Reward: Breakfast with Trump in his apartment

Boardroom: Stephanie, Alex, Chris S.

Fired: Stephanie

American Eagle Outfitters

Task: Design a new "wearable technology" fashion line.

Winning Team: Magna
Tana (project manager), Bren, Craig, Kendra

Losing Team: Net Worth
Alex (project manager), Angie, Chris S.

Alex is so eager to get to the drafting table that he forgets to research his market. There's no such mistake in the Magna camp as Tana and Kendra conduct a focus group in an American Eagle retail store and learn which gadgets their customers use and how they'd like to see them incorporated into clothing. Alex gives Chris just one thing to do—purchase gear at Best Buy—and he botches it by leaving his credit card on the counter. Angie realizes that most of the responsibility is on her shoulders and when the team leaves a jacket behind during a mad dash to their presentation her cool exterior crumbles.

Reward: A shopping spree at Bergdorf Goodman

Boardroom: Alex, Angie, Chris S.

Fired: Angie

Pontiac Solstice

Task: Create a marketing brochure for GM's newest car.

Winning Team: Magna
Kendra (project manager), Craig, Tana

Losing Team: Net Worth
Chris S. (project manager), Alex, Bren

The Net Worth men cackle with glee when they realize that the task is about cars and they're up against a team that's dominated by women. Sure enough, Magna looks to be in trouble when Tana and Craig go to bed early and leave Kendra in the lurch. But Kendra pulls off a brilliant solo performance and blows the boys away with a brochure so good that GM adopts it for use in its nation-wide campaign. Meanwhile, Chris' leadership is as unfocused as the oddly blurry photo on the team's opening page.

Reward: Meet with Isiah Thomas and several New York Knicks on the floor of Madison Square Garden

Boardroom: Chris S., Alex, Bren

Fired: Chris S.

Staples

Task: Create a new product to reduce office clutter.

Winning Team: Magna
Craig (project manager), Kendra, Tana

Losing Team: Net Worth
Alex (project manager), Bren

It's more of the same on both sides as Alex sketches out his own idea without any input from Staples executives or a focus group, while Magna conducts methodical market research in a retail store. The results are predictable: Magna's rotating cube with multiple storage compartments impresses the execs and office managers at their presentation, while Net Worth's Packrat, a table on wheels with a hinged transparent lid, elicits only head scratching. Craig and Kendra's rapidly deteriorating relationship is the only blemish on an otherwise sparkling Magna performance. Alex squeaks by again when the homesick Bren falls on his sword during their boardroom battle.

Reward: Breakfast with George and Carolyn at the legendary Rainbow Room

Boardroom: Alex, Bren

Fired: Bren

Hanes T-Shirt

Task: Design a commemorative limited edition T-shirt.

Winning Team: Magna
Kendra (project manager), Craig

Losing Team: Net Worth
Tana (project manager), Alex

Net Worth's wildly successful collaboration with artist Burton Morris goes down the drain when Tana decides that shopping for rhinestones in Staten Island is more important than figuring out a marketing strategy. Meanwhile, Kendra's e-mail blast to Magna artist Romero Britto's fan base turns a T-shirt sale into an art world event. For her reward, Kendra dons the snuggest flight suit anyone's seen since George W. Bush's landing on that Persian Gulf aircraft carrier and scores yet another victory by symbolically blowing Craig out of the sky. In the boardroom, too much time spent in Washington, D.C. dooms Alex when The Donald catches him using voodoo arithmetic to put a better spin on his win/loss record.

Reward: A simulated dogfight in actual fighter planes

Boardroom: Tana, Alex

Fired: Alex

Interviews/Video Game Championship/ Athlete Challenge

Task: Interview with four business luminaries. Take charge of a special event.

Video Game Championship Team: Kendra, Danny, Erin, Michael

Athlete Challenge Team: Tana, Brian, Chris S., Kristen

Season three's interview gauntlet features David Brandon (Chairman & CEO, Domino's Pizza, Inc.), Darlene Daggett (President, U.S. Commerce, QVC, Inc.), Howard Lorber (Chairman, Prudential Douglas Elliman Real Estate), and Greg Brenneman (Chairman & CEO, Burger King Corp.). After questioning the remaining applicants, they have a question for Trump: what's Craig doing here? He's promptly fired. Kendra and Tana are all smiles until they meet their finale teams: Kendra gets the "scatterbrains"—Danny, Michael, and Erin—and Tana the "three stooges"—Brian, Chris, and Kristen. Kendra tries to stay positive as she takes on the Video Game World Championship Tournament, but Danny's dim-witted ditty to appalled clients outs her pout. Kendra rallies, but at what school did the last of the Book Smarts learn that it's okay to put an important sponsor's displays in a dingy basement next to the toilets and stuffed animal heads? Meanwhile, Tana at the NYC 2012 Athlete Challenge, knows she's sitting on top of a giant powder keg—and when Kristen announces "I don't give a [bleep]. My ass is no longer on the line," we know the fuse has been lit. (Continued . . .)

Boardroom: Craig, Kendra, Tana
Fired: Craig